The Dynamics of Urbanism

The Dynamics of Urbanism

Dr Peter F. Smith

Director, Design and Psychology Research Unit
and Senior Lecturer University of Sheffield

HUTCHINSON EDUCATIONAL

Hutchinson Educational Ltd
3 Fitzroy Square, London W 1

London Melbourne Sydney Auckland
Wellington Johannesburg Cape Town
and agencies throughout the world

First published 1974
© P. F. Smith 1974

Set in Monophoto Times
by BAS Printers Limited, Wallop, Hampshire

Printed in Great Britain by The Anchor Press Ltd
and bound by Wm Brendon & Sons Ltd, both of
Tiptree, Essex

ISBN 0 09 119780 5 (cased)
          119781 3 (paper)

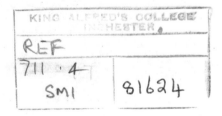

Contents

Acknowledgements

I gratefully acknowledge help from the psychologist Dr Peter Warr who was not totally discouraging after reading the first draft, to Dr Philip Seager who made many constructive suggestions for the final script, and to my Secretary, Mrs Margaret Prince, who displayed a patience usually reserved for the gods. Thanks are also due to the University of Sheffield for helping to finance my travels.

Preface

Architecture is not really a discipline, and its exponents generally have no loyalty to any particular world view. A good architect has exceptionally good peripheral vision. Anything is legitimate which generates a design image. Le Corbusier may transmute a sea shell into a pilgrimage church. All visual events are fair game to the creative mind.

As I am an architect, it is perhaps understandable that I should bring these scavanging techniques to bear upon the problem of the nature of human reactions to built environment.

Purists within the disciplines from which I freely steal ideas may be horrified with an attitude they would consider grossly simplistic. It is likely that charges of heresy will be laid from many quarters. I will attempt to console myself with the belief that the path to deeper understanding in any sphere of thought is paved with heresies. Indeed one can imagine Marshall McCluhan suggesting that one proceed by means of small heresies to the grand truth. But perhaps that is just the hubris inherent in most architects.

'Urbanism' is a portmanteau term which embraces the concept of architecture in its external and internal manifestations as well as the wider aspects of townscape. Perception of urbanism does not recognize intellectual compartments and so this discourse will leap across traditional boundaries with equal agility.

PETER F. SMITH
September 1974

Note

All the illustrations and photographs – with a few exceptions which are individually and separately acknowledged – were produced and prepared specially for *The Dynamics of Urbanism* by the author.

1 Towns and Cities for Real People

What matters to inhabitants of cities, apart from fundamentals such as the availability of work and essential services, is the quality of buildings and the in-between spaces they generate. All the right strategic decisions may be made, and the planning theory be impeccable, but if the physical consequences, the actual objects in space, do not add up to a satisfying and vigorous environment, good feasibility decision-making is of no consequence. In the present arrangement of things, armies of planners seem to be engaged in the scientific aspects of the urban design agenda. But things so often go wrong at the last stage. New towns are, to varying degrees, deficient in that indefinable quality called *urbanism*. Things are even worse in the sphere of urban renewal. All towns and cities have their share of high prestige, low satisfaction urban non-events. Perhaps this is because we do not know what urbanism really is, in the psychological sense.

The phenomenology of towns and cities has been low in the order of priorities, partly because value in this context cannot be quantified. A further reason may be that it is not really seen to matter. People are thought to have limited capacity when it comes to appreciating built environment. Possibly human beings are more sensitive to environmental quality than administrators and politicians have ever conceded. Evidence for this is found in the conservationist backlash which is now sweeping the country, and the proliferation of urban action groups, resurrecting the spirit of the Skeffington Report.[1]

All this has particular relevance to places, the economically grey areas, which are endeavouring to attract inhabitants. Maybe the quality of life which is offered by northern towns and cities in Britain is a significant disincentive to immigration from the more environmentally-conscious south. If urban phenomenology can be seen to have economic relevance, then there is a chance the order of priorities for finance and effort will be modified in its favour. Cities in grey areas can become magnets for industry and commerce if, in their policy of renewal, they opt for nothing less than excellence. In saying this it must be remembered that equally as important as buildings is the space between them and the use to which it is designated. Urban excellence may help to turn the economic tide in favour of depressed areas. This immediate problem gives a sharper cutting-edge to the argument. However there are wider issues.

If the estimate that 80 per cent of the population of the developed world will be accommodated in towns and cities by A.D. 2000 is correct, there will need to be considerable and rapid town-making. As an area of study, urbanism is extremely popular. In Britain, specialized centres are appearing regularly, many of them manifesting a geographical bias. There is intense activity within those spheres of urbanism which yield to examination by measurement. Perhaps understandably in an academic climate which equates science with measurement, there is little being said about the unquantifiable factors which affect urban life. Yet the un-quantifiable things may well have the major influence upon demeanour within the urban milieu.

There is a need for ideas which emerge from the interface between psychology and philosophy, art and technology, and this book un-ashamedly crosses boundaries in an effort to isolate the nature of the appeal of towns and cities. A design strategy which recognizes the importance of the quality of visual events should have immeasurably beneficial consequences at the tactical level.

As urban quality has much to do with perception and evaluation, psychological theory will figure in the discourse. This inevitably involves hazards for those who dip into such deep waters from an alien shore, especially if their only qualification involves possessing some of its raw material. To some the argument may appear too speculative, and because speculation is not readily testable, it is deemed to be outside the scope of serious consideration. This, of course, was how radio and penicillin were discovered.

Whilst the method is descriptive, a ground-beat of polemic may, from time to time, be discernible. For this is being written in the belief that the visual art of building cities has not caught up with the functional and transportation agenda. Towns and cities may be increasingly sophisti-cated in meeting technical needs but now is the time to bring deeper human needs into the brief.

There is enormous potential in the ingredients of towns and cities to stimulate and excite the mind, to break down person-to-person and person-to-city alienation. Third millennium man will have to contend with many problems. It is the responsibility of present-day planners and architects to ensure that the city is not one of them.

This is being written in the space between European Conservation Year and European Architectural Heritage Year. That fact is coincidental but useful.

Conservation Year focussed attention upon the malign effects of pollu-tion, and drew attention to its more discreet forms. Pollution can attack the visual field in terms of the way man shapes or mis-shapes his environment. Glass, steel and concrete monuments to sterile imaginations, erupting between those precious interstices between urban motorways, rank high among contemporary pollutants.

European Architectural Heritage Year, we hope, will encourage re-assessment of historic towns and cities. In the course of this present discussion, frequent reference is made to historic places, not because of their historicity, but because they offer many useful similes and analogies for the contemporary architect and urban designer. Existing towns are the matrix from which new concepts of urbanism must emerge.

Conserving a heritage does not mean petrifying it but developing and maximizing it. Building is necessary in a world of exploding population. It is not sufficient simply to complain about visual vandalism. The suggestion made here is that low standards of urban design are in part the consequence of a gross under-estimation of the complexities of human perception and mental need. It may contribute to higher standards of design if the mode of response of the mind to built environment is understood in terms of values, symbolism and aesthetics.

The human brain is a system, and as such yields to a measure of analysis regarding its needs and mode of operation. A system may be defined as a 'special universe' in which certain rules operate to achieve a number of well-defined aims. It is a system within a system, within a system . . . . A crucial related system is the external environment, the urban part of which is the concern of this study. A number of psychologists have been saying quite loudly that the inferior built environment which is being imposed on society is debilitating human minds in parallel with the physical effects of atmospheric pollution.[2]

Awareness of the creative possibilities latent in the urban milieu must depend upon experience. Creativity is a function of memory. Before it is possible to create there must be a wide vocabulary of perceptual experience which is the essential matrix from which the new may emerge. Thus memory is a key factor in this operation, and memory only records what has been perceived.

The aim is to suggest how perception is achieved by the brain and to note how the natural mode of operation of the memory system imposes restrictions upon perception. Experiencing environment is a creative act. It depends as much upon the subject interpreting the visual array as upon the disposition of the objects in space. Professor Terence Lee makes clear that distinction between subject and object: 'It is not merely the objects on the ground but their *subjective representation* in people's minds that governs the forms of human-behaviour.'[3] It also governs their mental demeanour, with therapeutic or baleful consequences. Environment is never neutral, it is invariably a 'hidden persuader' for good or ill. It was a great shock to planners and other philanthropists when hygienic, prairified New Towns gave birth to a new medical phenomenon, 'New

Town neurosis'. The sad thing about Utopian planners is that their design agenda tends to exclude real people, substituting theoretical constructs which support a dream. So this is not a prescription for Utopia. It will not make design in urbanism any easier. The aim is to delineate more finely the design agenda in architecture and urbanism.

Part One discusses in general terms the biological and psychological aspects of perception which are directly relevant to built environment. It describes three levels upon which the urban milieu may be perceived, namely:

1. cognitive perception; the recognition of urban objects by consensus features such as style or function.
2. perception of levels of symbolic overlay to urban events from the personal to the collective levels.
3. relational perception which is concerned with visually expressed value-systems, in terms both of formal relationships within a style, or more abstract relationships appertaining to the broader townscape.

Part Two considers the policy which should be adopted by designers within the urban context. It does this largely by illustrating the psychologically satisfying potential behind the very fact of a town or city. This concerns the passive, dynamic, and symbolic design agendas.

Part Three attempts to outline a design strategy which capitalizes on the diverse facilities of the human mind.

References

1. *Committee on Public Participation in Planning* (the Skeffington Report), (London, 1969)
2. See, for example, A. E. Parr, 'City and psyche', *Yale Review*, autumn (1965), 71–85; and Rapoport and Kantor, 'Complexity and ambiguity in environmental design', *Journal of the American Institute of Planners*, July (1967)
3. T. Lee, in a paper delivered at Newcastle University

Part One
The Complexities of Perception

2 Formation of an Urban Schema

Perception is the use of memory to make sense of phenomena and, if necessary, calculate the requisite motor responses needed to negotiate the objects in space.

Three functions of the central nervous system contribute to the totality of perception

> Motivation
> Memory
> Learning

Motivation

The emergent human being has a compelling need to make sense of his environment. Initially the paramount drives are linked to the hunger need, and the infant soon learns the tactile and topographical qualities of that special part of his environment which pays off in terms of food. This information impresses itself in the memory not necessarily through an innate ability to perceive, but through detailed experimentation to learn the location and shape of this very rewarding part of his little cosmos. Seeing is an intrinsic ability; perception is largely, but not perhaps exclusively, a learned ability. It is a commonplace to say that 'we need to see', but it would be more accurate to conclude that 'we see what we need'. Without motivation there would be no perception. If homeostatic equilibrium were maintained within the infant by some ingenious mechanism, as is the case when the infant is in the womb, it would have no incentive to make sense of the chaos that bombards the receptors. External environment only has reality because the brain has specific needs and has learnt that certain combinations of light and shadow, texture and perspective, have a three-dimensional probability in relation to those needs. This, however, is merely inference based on past experiences which only *suggests* that visual phenomena obey certain rules.

Space is one of the abstract schemata we impose on our world in order to make experience more coherent and meaningful.[1]

This 'communication between environment and the mind' is therefore not by direct transfer.

The body is equipped with a number of highly sensitive receptors which convert energy emitted by the environment into energy of a different nature which conforms to the structural code of the brain; it converts the language of environment into the language of the cortex. And there is no point-to-point correspondence. The brain does not automatically make sense of the external, phenomenal world.

To a large degree William James's oft-quoted assertion that environment is intrinsically '. . . a big, blooming, buzzing confusion' is still true. That this is not the entire truth has been indicated by Noam Chomsky who refers to 'universal archetypes of language'.

In the area of visual perception, the images which fall on the retina are upside-down, inverted from left to right, and distorted by being projected onto the concave surface of the retina. At this point the energy transfer takes place; the light energy is converted to brain impulses which pass along the optic nerve to the visual cortex.

First, then, come needs which in turn produce motives which lead to drives. In the process of gaining drive satisfaction, the infant learns the rules of primary perception – perception of the basic three-dimensional probability of the environment. Here it is useful to quote E. J. Murray's distinction between motives and drives:

A motive is 'an internal factor that arouses, directs and integrates a person's behaviour'.
A drive 'refers to the internal process that goads a person into action'.[2]

In a child the first drives are homeostatic, that is, they are orientated towards satisfaction of organic needs, and are engendered by a built-in preference for equilibrium within the organism. Soon, however, other motives begin to operate, especially those produced by the exploratory drive. The organic drives are sometimes termed 'biogenic' and the exploratory drives 'psychogenic'.[3]

Psychogenic drives are infinite in their variety. As an individual gains control over the means of satisfying biogenic needs, more and more attention is allocated to the satisfaction of secondary, psychogenic needs. In one person they may be harnessed to achieving power, wealth or status; in another the goal may be some physical feat of strength and endurance, in a third it may be a supreme work of art. It is the same pattern of drives which inspires a Michelangelo or a Machiavelli.

If the need becomes extreme or obsessive, then the visual evidence may become grossly distorted or falsified during the process of perception. The mirage is the brain compensating for the absence of civilization to one lost in the desert. The mind is quite capable of constructing fantasies if reality becomes intolerable.

It is an acknowledged characteristic of the brain that it has two opposed tendencies, one promoting analysis and order, the other seeking new combinations of patterns – novelty – surprise. These polarized facilities of the brain reflect the inhibitory/excitatory modes of the nervous system.

The two opposite principles operating within the human mind result in a tension which is an important motivating factor influencing thought and perception. Because this tensile equation is of such importance in the matter of perception and design, it is desirable to examine the characteristics of each tendency.

In the first place, there is the principle which binds man to the rest of nature, that of homeostasis. It has earlier been indicated that this principle operates on the physiological level. Now it is accepted that the principle also applies to purely mental functions and is manifest in a desire for harmony and balance, order and stability, within environment.

This aspect of mentation is related to the analysing, dissecting side of the psyche which inspires the desire to make phenomena conform to a ready-made pattern. Because it is a tendency to reduce experience to fit existing patterns, and because it manifests the activity of the focussing, ordering side of the psyche, it is a part of what is called the 'convergent' pattern of behaviour. In personality theory it materializes as the introvert tendency. Ultimately the goal of mental homeostasis is nirvana, the final stage of non-being, the logical end of the inhibitory tendency of the system.

Clearly there has to be a counterbalance to such a tendency, otherwise humanity would rapidly disappear into the eye of its own vortex. George Miller indicates that there are two complementary principles which govern behaviour:

An organism works to reduce its primary drives, to bring its tensions to an absolute minimum, to return to homeostatic equilibrium. If social motives are learnt by primary drives, it seems reasonable to assume that they will also manifest this self-terminating characteristic. When this pattern of tension reduction is imposed on social motives, however, it leads to an odd distortion. The simple truth is that social action does not always reduce tensions. To imply that it must suggests that persistent diligence and hard work are symptoms of maladjustment . . . that nirvana is the only goal that anyone could imagine in this life. But this is nonsense. No sane person would reduce all his motives to a minimum . . . Instead, when homeostasis gives us a chance, we constantly seek out new tensions to keep us occupied and entertained.[4]

So, there is another side to the system, which is really a system in its own right. In motivational theory it is called intrinsic motivation, probably because both the need and the goal are cerebral. In Koestler's words: 'The main incentive to its exploratory activities are novelty, surprise, conflict, uncertainty.'[5]

This links up with the theme propounded by G. A. Miller:

Surprise is an essential to mental health and growth . . . It is not enough merely to have energy falling on our eyes, ears, skin and other receptors; the critical thing is that the pattern of these energies must keep changing in unforeseen ways.[6]

For several millennia these bi-polar activating principles have been recognized and it has been acknowledged that life is something of a tight-rope stretched between the poles. This is indicated by Spinks:

The reconciliation of opposites within an extended historical context constitutes one of the main themes of religious and historical movements. The Yin-Yang of the Chinese, the personification of Rta in the Rig Veda, the principle of the unification of opposites, the existence of Mitra and Varuna, the two guardians in Hindu mythology, and the concept of Tao, each represents . . . a metaphysical example of the complimentariness of opposed attitudes.[7]

To Freud these opposites were irreconcilable, inducing 'an eternal conflict between two distinct and completely opposed forces, one seeking to preserve and extend life, the other seeking to reduce life to the inorganic state out of which it arose.' This conflict between drives aimed at 'the life proper to the species' and those directed towards what may ultimately be called the 'death-wish' was defined in desperation by Freud as 'the dialectic of neurosis'.

Spinks makes wider claims for the operational significance of these binary drives:

The programme of the libido as exhibited in the activities of the personal psyche is also the programme of civilization . . . The history of the individual, the community or the race is conditioned by the bi-polar nature of libido which 'incites' man to new and creative activities, and also permits him to sink into periods of seemingly uncreative inertia . . .[8]

Thus mental homeostasis is kept in check by the area of need which calls for new and ever-changing sensations. These exploratory and teleological drives which hunger for new patterns of relationship and the primacy of the self over the group, stem, as mentioned, from intrinsic motivation. In one sense the tension between the two principles is between mind and organism, or as St Paul might have put it, spirit and flesh.

This tension is a characteristic of man's internal or intimate environment and as such it governs the mode of perception of external environment. Both perception and creation are profoundly influenced by the personal homeostatic/intrinsic motivation equation. Perception is almost as positive a process as creativity. 'Space is not seen but inferred', and the inference is an interpretation of the sensory information transmitted to the brain. Meaning is imposed on a situation. The values of the two sides of the equation are infinitely variable but the symbols in the equation remain constant. It is because there is this constant factor that it is possible to move from theory of personality to theory of perception.

C. G. Jung rounds off the argument which maintains that the natural thought and perception system is subject to bias which itself is the resultant of the personal homeostatic motivation/intrinsic motivation 'force system'. Using personality theory terms he says:

Introversion and extroversion, as a typical attitude, means an essential bias which conditions the whole psychic process, establishes the habitual reactions, and thus determines not only the style of behaviour, but also the *nature of subjective experience*.[9]

Koestler sees this as a universal fact of existence:

On every level of the evolutionary hierarchy, stability is maintained by the equilibration of forces pulling in opposite directions: one asserting the part's independence, autonomy, individuality, the other keeping it in its place as a dependent unit of the whole.[10]

The bi-polarity of human mentation is attributed by some to the physical structure of the brain. In a medical paper delivered in 1964, Professor Paul MacLean stated:

Man finds himself in the predicament that Nature has endowed him essentially with three brains which, despite great differences in structure, must function together and communicate with one another. The oldest of these brains is essentially reptilian. The second has been inherited from lower mammals, and the third is a late mammalian development, which in its culmination in primates, has made man peculiarly man.[11]

Operationally, the two older brains are classified together as the primitive or limbic brain, and enjoy a high degree of autonomy. It is a curious fact that nature chose not to develop these brains, but to superimpose upon them a new brain, the neo-cortex, which has developed at remarkable speed. This system is responsible for 'higher' mental functions, rational thought, verbal ability, etc. The limbic brain controls the visceral functions of the body, but it also performs two other roles which have considerable bearing upon the total performance of the mind.

First, the limbic brain generates deep-rooted responses which are concerned with emotions. It can, it seems, even respond to non-verbal symbols. Secondly, it contains the mechanism which is responsible for conscious arousal, and so can exercise considerable influence upon the neo-cortex. The significance of this will be considered later.

Some writers go so far as to consider this uneasy cohabitation of two different brains as a flaw in evolution. Koestler quotes it as 'schizophysiology'[12] which is very much in line with Freud's 'dialectic of neurosis'.

Without doubt, man is a paradoxical creature, and the relative strengths of each psychological principle which might emanate from the two brains decides a motivational bias which unconsciously colours perception. This is the bias of the personality equation which imposes a selective filter upon mental processing.

References

1. G. A. Miller, *Psychology: The Science of Mental Life*, Hutchinson (1964)
2 E. J. Murray, *Motivation and Emotion*, Prentice-Hall (1964)
3 J. L. Fuller, *Motivation a Biological Perspective*, Random House (New York, 1962)
4 G. A. Miller, *op. cit.* p. 269
5 A. Koestler, *The Act of Creation*, Hutchinson (1964), p. 507
6 G. A. Miller, *op. cit.* p. 34
7 G. S. Spinks, *Psychology and Religion*, Methuen (1963), p. 57
8 G. S. Spinks, *op. cit.* pp. 55, 56
9 C. G. Jung, *Modern Man in Search of a Soul*, Kegan Paul (1933)
10 A. Koestler, *op. cit.*
11 P. MacLean 'Contrasting functions of limbic and neocortical aspects of medicine', *American Journal of Medicine*, **XXV** (4), (1958), 611–26
12 A. Koestler, *The Ghost in the Machine*, Pan Books (1970), p. 325 (first published: Hutchinson, 1967)

3 The Memory System

There is no neater definition than de Bono's 'A memory is what is left behind when something happens and does not completely unhappen.'[1] Perception is based on memory, because it is impossible to perceive phenomena which are not partially related to past experiences. Consequently the mechanics of memory are an important aspect of this examination.

There are three kinds of storage: short-term, medium, and long-term or permanent. Flexner, Flexner and Roberts proposed, in 1966, that short-term memory is dependent 'upon the reverberation of neuronal impulses'.[2] Medium-term storage 'may be based upon changes in the concentration of ions or small molecules or on changes in the configuration or location of pre-existing macro-molecules'. This type of memory lasts one or two days, and may be an intermediate stage in the establishment of long-term memory.

Long-term memory is 'dependent upon DNA-directed synthesis of protein' which is involved in the creation of new synaptic connections between cells as well as changes within the neurons themselves.

Whatever the tenure of storage, the principle involved is the same, namely, the connection between cells. This is called the 'interneuronal' theory of memory. There is another theory which claims that memory is encoded chemically within neurons, perhaps in the form of specific molecules of ribonucleic acid (RNA). This is termed the 'intraneuronal' theory, and seems to be declining in credibility. On the basis of the interneuronal theory, the brain consists of some 10 000 million cells, and each cell is capable of establishing some 5000 connections, so it is clear the storage potential of the system is impressive. Even the most advanced intelligence only fractionally exploits the resources of the brain.

When considering types of memory, for present purposes it is sufficient to reduce the problem to short-term and long-term. The former is vital to the process of perception. The brain can only concentrate on a small attention fragment at one time. The eye makes rapid scanning movements and the brain holds the information from these attention fragments for a short time. It is this holding effect which enables the brain to perceive coherence in environment. It is analogous to the after-glow on a radar screen. As the strobe moves round the screen it picks up objects which glow on the sensitized surface of the cathode ray tube for a few seconds. This enables them to be related to other 'blips' which appear further round the screen. The result is a 'picture', a coherent pattern which bears a direct relationship to objects in space. However, there is no point-to-point correspondence, and the information has to be interpreted. The operator perceives through an electronic system. The blips represent reality, but they have been converted into the code of that system. It is a close analogy to the system of perception employed by the brain.

The brain perceives in fragments. Short-term memory enables these fragments to be linked together. Two subsequent perception fragments may be as shown below.

and

Units of information

Short-term memory enables the relationship to be established in the following way.

Coherent element of information

Perhaps the most obvious facility of short-term memory is manifest in language. Coherence depends on the composition of groups of words which relate to the experience of another person, and sense depends on the ability to relate together the beginning, middle and end of a sentence.

Long-term memory is established by connections between cells to form patterns. Donald Hebb was one of the first to suggest that long-term storage is achieved by the physical changes in the brain involving linkages between cells.[3] Steven Rose has shown that RNA and proteins are used in establishing such connections. Experiments with animals exposed to concentrated problem-solving situations indicated a significant rise in the RNA and protein content of the brain. Thus, a long-term memory may be described as a permanent trace on the brain which consists of the physical connection of perception fragments to form a coherent memory pattern. The process of establishing a trace was described by Richard Semon as early as 1921 as 'engramming'. A pattern of engrams recording a unit of information has been termed a 'metacircuit'. A group of connected cells may be graphically represented by an engram line. This is a useful form of notation for describing the behaviour of the memory surface and is represented by a simple line symbolizing cells linked together.

Basis of engram notation

Using the engram notation a keyhole metacircuit would be as shown here.

Metacircuit in engram terms

Whilst it is now generally conceded that long-term storage involves a metabolic change, there are two schools of thought as to how storage is achieved through the interlacement of cells and nerve pathways. One theory is that, in a sense, all knowledge pre-exists in the brain, and perception and thought are a matter of internal discovery.

A permanent impress involves giving extra emphasis to a pattern of cells and pathways, so that it stands out as figure against ground.*

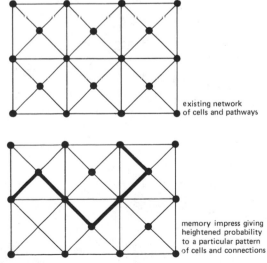

existing network
of cells and pathways

memory impress giving
heightened probability
to a particular pattern
of cells and connections

Cell pattern hypothesis[4]

* A view propounded by Niels Jerne of Frankfurt.

The other theory proposes that long-term memory involves the formation of new linkages.

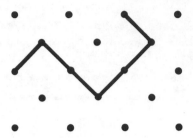

Cell pattern hypothesis[4]

Spatially, there have been numerous models produced, but the one which is most consistent with current knowledge has emerged from mathematicians. Until fairly recently it was believed that the brain stored material in the pigeon-hole manner of a computer. This turned out to be too simple, because a memory has the property of somehow being diffused throughout the brain. A unit of memory comprises a pattern of cells and nerve pathways which cohere into an encoded version of the events of the memory. However, these cells are available for use by other impressed data. So memory patterns are intertwined in a wondrously complex way.

In 1969 a group at Edinburgh University, led by Longuet-Higgins, produced a mathematical model of diffused memory storage.[4]

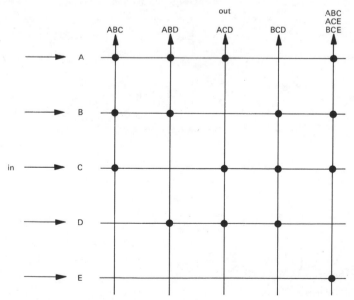

Information processing hypothesis[4]

The memory comprises the pattern of dots and connections. A particular combination of incoming signals produces an output (recall) signal along the vertical axis which is fully matched to that combination. It should be noted that one combination of input signals can stimulate more than one output signal. On the other hand, a particular output signal can be produced by different incoming combinations.

Recently, a model of storage has been proposed which relates it to holography, a by-product of laser research. If a photographic plate is exposed to an object illuminated by a coherent laser light beam, the result on the developed plate is an encoded version of the object which bears no configurative correspondence with it. This is a hologram. However, if this hologram is viewed in laser light a three-dimensional picture of the object appears.

What is so remarkable about this technique is that if the plate is broken even the smallest fragment, when seen in laser light, will reveal a recognizable version of the whole object. Somehow the picture is diffused over the whole surface of the plate.

The neuronal process involved in establishing memory also, it seems, displays holographic characteristics, and new insight into mental storage seems to be emerging from the mathematical basis of laser photography.

This does not invalidate the principle of engramming, but it does mean that a memory pattern is very much a three-dimensional affair. Whilst it will have a strong centre, it nevertheless reverberates through many parts of the brain. The notation of the engram line serves a useful purpose in this context, provided it is remembered that it represents the ultimate in simplification.

Learning

In the early years of mental development, basic patterns and pathways are established, as the elementary model of the world is constructed. They are a physical, internal representation of external reality. Each basic category may be called a *schema*. These schemas will be modified by extension, but rarely do they change their infrastructure. It has been necessary to go into the physiology of memory to emphasize the importance of these basic schemas in providing a life-long datum of perception. The brain is a physical model of experience, and this is how it is to be understood when considering cognitive assessment of the built milieu.

It is now a commonplace to say that perception is largely – some would still say, exclusively – a matter of learning. Environment is physically negotiated by reference to what is already known. Past experience enables the mind to establish probabilities about the visual array. The same goes for perception on the 'higher' intellectual level. A particular street is recognized because the memory has established a pattern of cell connections and linking pathways which is an encoded version of the visual events of that street. Fortunately the memory 'bank' is built up irrespective of conscious awareness. Studies in subliminal perception lead to the conclusion that data can be perceived, classified, and even responded to, without reference to conscious attention. The term 'subliminal perception' is used throughout to mean perception below the level of consciousness in the general sense, and not in the limited sense of a stimulus presented for such a brief period of time that it evades conscious awareness.

When a new street is encountered, the classification procedure begins. If there is enough about it which is recognizable this transaction may be carried out unconsciously. A street in a foreign country is a different matter. Conscious attention takes a hand in relating external reality to internal models. The urban events are able to be processed because, though on a superficial level they are unfamiliar, there is usually much more below the surface which coincides with schemas of memory.

The process of building-up the matrix of memory is far from constant. During childhood and adolescence there is an information implosion. First of all, basic concepts are categorized, and then there is increasing discrimination towards differentiation within categories. Basic schemas of memory are enriched by detail. This applies to all areas of learning, including the conceptualization of built environment. The process may be represented by a graph.

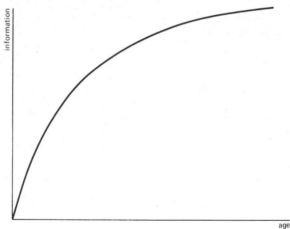

Rate of information input

Inevitably the pace of input slackens as an individual becomes habituated to his environment.

An important component of the recording system is the *classifier*. This enables urban visual input to be perceived and classified according to its conformity with the experiential schema. This is not so simple as it may appear. Schemas interconnect and coincide at many points. A church is part of the general urban schema. At the same time it is likely to be part of the schema of religion. When it comes to evaluation there may be a conflict of schemas. A church with a spire and all the other familiar cues may give satisfaction on the level of the urban schema. Theologically it may represent an obsolete symbol-system which inhibits the development of Christianity.[5] Indeed a building or piece of environment may mark a crossroads of several schemas, which is just one source of the complexity behind perception and response.

Schemas divide into numerous sub-schemas, rather like the branching out of a tree. To a child, a house is as pictured here.

Basic house image

This is the basic house schema. As experience develops, the schema is extended into sub-categories such as terraced house, semi-detached, etc. Ultimately it crosses time and space to embrace historical and modern houses at home and abroad. The extent of the sub-division is a matter of experience and, to some degree, conscious learning. The church schema begins with the image shown here;

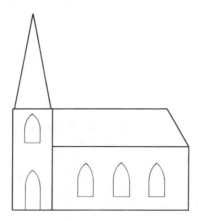

Basic church image

27

but may end by embracing anything from A.D. 320 to the present. It may accommodate subtleties such as the ability to recognize an architect or the hand of a particular sculptor.

In terms of engram notation this means the simple addition of an attention pattern to the appropriate category pattern established in the memory surface.

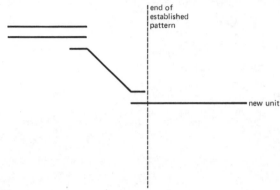

end of
established
pattern

new unit

Adding to schema in engram notation

When a set of cues are received by the brain, the appropriate sub-schema is automatically selected and attention flows across the sub-schema, relating the new impression to the established pattern, and modifying the pattern where necessary.

Furthermore, learning involves establishing relationships between patterns, so that the internal model comes to reflect something of the complexity of external events. Even so, basic patterns still remain, and indeed become more emphasized as the nerve pathway communication system becomes increasingly extensive.

In engram notation, two basic, unrelated patterns may exist as shown below.

Engram diagram

As experience adds to the schemas of memory, the picture may become altered to that shown on the facing page.

The two patterns are still identifiable as figure against ground, but at the same time are integrated into a wider cortical system.

All the basic categories of information within this area of study, the schemas, contribute to what may be termed the *macroschema* of urban

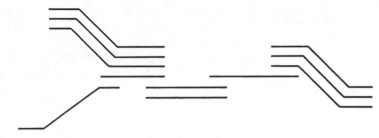

Engram diagram

form. The accumulated experience of houses, churches, shopping streets, town squares, etc. comprises an active pattern which forms the datum of perception within the urban situation.

References

1 E. de Bono, *The Mechanism of Mind*, Jonathan Cape (1969), p. 41
2 Cited in *Neuronal Changes that May Store Memory*, Documenta Geigy, Basle
3 D. Hebb, *The Organisation of Behaviour* (New York, 1973)
4 Cited in N. Calder, *The Mind of Man*, BBC Publications (1970), p. 130
5 P. F. Smith, *Third Millennium Churches*, Galliard (1973)

4 Subliminal Perception

Some elementary principles of perception were the concern of the first chapters. This paves the way for the next stage in the transaction between mind and environment, the response. Just as important as a system of storage is the pattern of retrieval.

Earlier it was suggested that information is diffused through the brain. The operational effects of such a system were recognized long before current mathematical models were conceived. In the 1920s a psychologist, F. C. Bartlett, proposed that data carried by the system act in concert, not as individual units. Bartlett gives a further definition to the concept of the schema by describing it as

an active organization of past reactions, or past experiences which must always be supposed to be operating in any well-adapted organic response. That is, whenever there is any order or regularity of behaviour, a particular response is possible only because it is related to other responses which have been serially organized, yet which operate not simply as individual members coming one after another, but as a unitary mass.[1]

Bartlett was concerned here with the stored information which makes possible an appropriate motor-response to a given set of environmental cues. Life would be impossible if the brain had consciously to formulate a detailed muscular programme each time one foot is placed above and in front of the other as stairs are climbed. However, this model is equally appropriate to the whole field of storage and response in environment. The schema is a useful analogy.

Recognition and assimilation of visual events is not a simple matter. Superficially it would seem to be merely a question of equating external events with the internal model. If there is a sufficient area of correspondence, the classifier makes an appropriate designation to a schema. The unfamiliar elements are added to the schema so that the library of perceptual experience is expanded. The schema concept of Bartlett offers a useful model of how response is achieved. Recognition of an object involves the whole experiential schema which, though serially built-up, acts as 'a unitary mass'.

This is the ideal situation but it tends to be distorted by two major factors:

1. certain features of the memory-recall mechanism;
2. the complexities of personality.

Learning to Sleepwalk in Cities

During the years of information implosion, much of the learning process is conducted on the conscious level. The rate of information assimilation gradually levels-off as perception is increasingly monopolized by the familiar. Finally, learning tends to go underground.

It is hurtful to the ego of architects and planners, but the sad fact is that perhaps up to 90 per cent of the familiar built milieu remains unperceived by the conscious mind of the average urban dweller. Subliminal perception first came to public notice as a sinister form of conditioning, expertly exploited by ice-cream manufacturers in their sub-threshold cinema advertisments. The fact of subliminal perception has long been acknowledged. What is not so readily appreciated is that though it has certain important advantages it also possesses a sinister significance in relation to built environment – like the two aspects of Venus.

This is now emerging as a problem because of the form and character of the new environment of towns and cities. They bore. Because of their low frequency and variety of visual events, they make it easy for the mind to slip into subliminal gear, with conscious awareness merely focussed on avoiding hazards.

Such a state of affairs is not merely undesirable but positively harmful. As mentioned earlier, psychologists have been highlighting the malign social consequences of urban monotony. The reason why monotony is harmful is a complex question, and can only be described in outline here.

It is emerging that there are two systems of visual perception described as the 'primitive' and the 'classical'. At the International Congress of Psychology held in London in 1969, Dr Colwyn Trevarthan made this assertion:

The primitive complex optic system allows you to respond automatically to what's going on in the space around you as a whole. If something unexpected moves outside the central field of attention, it registers first through (the) second more primitive system before the classical visual system becomes aware of it.[2]

This is reinforced by conclusions drawn by Dr Norman Dixon of University College, London, who proposed in a paper last year that there could be two neural systems within the brain, 'one which yields specific information, and the other the capacity for conscious experience of this information'.[3]

A little physiology is required to amplify these statements. Conscious arousal is promoted by a dense cluster of cells around the brain stem which is known as the Reticular Activating System (RAS). Being so deep-rooted, it is part of the primitive or limbic brain.

The neocortex is essentially a brain developed for the *conscious experience* of sensory stimulation. There had to be a mechanism to control input to this limited capacity system so that it could be used to maximum advantage. This mechanism adapted to this use was the RAS. In effect the RAS exercises control over the cortex, monitoring signals from sense organs and selecting data worthy to receive conscious attention.

This poses two questions:

1. What happens to material not selected for conscious consideration?

2. Is the neocortex at the mercy of the limbic system since the regulator of consciousness is a part of this primitive brain?

Dixon would no doubt answer the first question by claiming that stimuli not promoted to consciousness nevertheless generate a complex reaction within the brain. He believes that:

at an early pre-conscious stage in cerebral processing, incoming information actually makes contact with memory systems, thereby *activating conceptual associates to the applied stimulus* . . . *sensory information can be received, classified and responded to without ever becoming conscious.*[4] [my italics]

Evidence to support the existence of subliminal perception comes from the neurologists who have been able to identify it in certain patients undergoing brain surgery while conscious. Through an electro-encephalograph (EEG) it is possible to measure the extent of neural activity prompted by external events and observe the point at which it crosses the threshold of consciousness. The gap between the first sign of neural activity and conscious awareness is appreciable enough to prove the validity of subliminal perception.

Dixon is quite sure that the deep-rooted mammalian portion of the brain containing the RAS 'can make complex discriminations without a contribution from those structures on which consciousness depends . . .'[5]

The significance of this theory should not be underrated. If material is 'classified' by the limbic brain, then it must possess information schemas to provide the context in which the classification procedure can operate. The belief is gaining strength that this information is not only experiential, but also refers to collective memory laid down at a time deep in pre-history and now structured within the brain: i.e. collective perceptual 'templates'. Paul MacLean, one of the pioneers of the 'three-brain' hypothesis, believes the limbic system:

might have the capacity to participate in a non-verbal type of symbolism. One might imagine, for example, that though the visceral brain (limbic brain) could never aspire to conceive of the colour red in terms of a three-letter word . . . it could associate the colour symbolically with such diverse things as blood, fainting, flowers, etc. – correlations leading to phobias, obsessive-compulsive behaviour, etc.[6]

The consequences of all this upon specifically architectural problems will be considered later on. In the meantime, a number of positive advantages stemming from such an arrangement are apparent.

First, this two-level perception system ensures that data allocated to conscious attention are of manageable proportions. Without such a discriminatory mechanism, the mind would soon collapse under sensory overload. At the same time, the much wider field of environment excluded from conscious consideration is nevertheless making an impact on the mind and is influencing attitude and strategy.

If only the consciously perceived data were to determine attitude and behaviour, the result would be a behavioural strategy based on an unrepresentative minority of external events. Input on the subliminal level ensures that the response to environment is balanced and not distorted by the unrepresentative portion consciously perceived.

The second advantage is that subliminal perception facilitates goal-orientated activity. For example, when the 'beam' of focal awareness is narrowed down by an overriding need, the mind is still able to react to the wider environment without prejudice to this focal acuity. For example, the conscious mind may be entirely absorbed by a problem at the office, yet it is possible to respond to all the complexities of urban environment on foot or in a car without conscious attention, so that the office is reached without awareness of the journey.

A third advantage concerns hazards. If everything in the visual milieu qualified for conscious attention, hazardous or inconsistent elements would not have prominence. Subliminal perception provides the necessary ground against which inconsistencies and hazards can stand out as figure. Focal awareness can then be directed to negotiating the hazard, or resolving the inconsistency.

The second question of prime importance concerned the relationship between the neocortex and its regulator, the RAS, located deep inside the limbic brain. There seems to be a logical contradiction inherent in a system in which the highly sophisticated neocortex is under the control of an evolutionary older mechanism. Insight into the style of operation of the RAS is offered by Madge and Arnold Scheibel writing in *The Neurosciences*:

Competition for the interest of the reticular arrays (RAS) must be high, and supremacy is gained for the moment in time only by those data that are most 'exotic' or compelling biologically . . . the core has limited patient and time-binding resources. Its logic is wide but superficial and its decisionary apparatus does not permit the luxury of hesitation.

33

So, on the face of it, the neocortex may be activated on the basis of the primitive 'logic' of the RAS. However, the system is not stable. Feedback loops ensure that there is two-way communication between the higher and lower brain, which means that one can influence the other. There is evidence that the neocortex enjoys a degree of initiative in this respect since it can determine its preferred level of activation. The higher brain can educate the limbic brain. A reasonably high level of intrinsic motivation ensures that the greater weight of traffic moves downwards, drawing the RAS closer into the milieu of higher logic.

Conversely, the more the overall style of perception is allowed to descend to the subliminal level the more powerful becomes the regime of the primitive brain. The ascending 'traffic' is dominant, meaning that the neocortex will increasingly adopt the criteria of the limbic system. It will show a preference for 'the exotic', things that glitter, and may come to non-rational conclusions such as 'size equals importance'.

Not surprisingly, Jonathan Sault 'wonders . . . how many of our behavioural reactions are processed outside the domains of the verbal centres . . . the seat of conscious awareness ("ratiocination")'.[7]

To summarize: it is coming to be accepted that there are two parallel systems of visual perception, the classical and the primitive. The latter by-passes consciousness to make direct contact with the primitive brain. The more this secondary, non-conscious system is allowed to dominate perception, the more response will be conditioned by primitive, non-rational criteria.[8]

Even with the most sophisticated human beings, these irrational criteria still register below the level of consciousness and effect conscious assessment. For example, in personnel selection matters a tall person has a bonus over one who is equally talented but less endowed with inches. Height and size are particular assets for politicians.

Underlying this whole proposition is the belief that the reticular formation is educable because of the feedback loops, making it possible for the neocortex, by its own executive control, to lower the threshold of arousal and thereby encourage the RAS to become progressively perceptive to subtlety and detail.

References

1 F. C. Bartlett, *Remembering*, Cambridge University Press (latest edition, 1957)
2 Quoted by J. Sault in *The Human Brain*, 'Doctor', 23 November (1972), p. 8
3 N. Dixon 'Who believes in subliminal perception?', *New Scientist*, 3rd February (1972), 252–55
4 N. Dixon, *op. cit.*
5 N. Dixon, *op. cit.* describes a range of experiments supporting the concept of subliminal perception.
6 Quoted by A. Koestler, *The Ghost in the Machine*, p. 326

7 J. Sault, *op. cit.*
8 A highly authoritative synoptic view of this field is provided by A. R. Luria, *The Working Brain*, Penguin Books (1973)

5 From Learning to Unlearning

There is a further characteristic of the brain which has profound consequences. It concerns another aspect of the mechanism of memory and recall. Perception is a matter of equating external events with internal, mental models. One facet of the mind looks for maximum compatability between the two, that is, the mental equivalent of the biological principle of homeostasis or the striving for equilibrium. In the mental sphere this implies balance between the real world and its representation within the brain. When this happens, subliminal perception can take over. This tendency to opt for the familiar is ably assisted by a further interesting characteristic of the memory-recall system. Whenever a pattern of memory is subject to recall, it undergoes a physiological change. Each time there is activation of a unit of memory, that unit becomes fractionally more sensitive to activation in the future. In other words it has a lower threshold or higher probability of excitation. In engram notation this situation is depicted by additional lines:

═══════════

What this means in perceptual terms is that events in the visual array which correspond to higher probability patterns of memory will tend to stand out as figure against ground. They push themselves to the front of the queue in the competition for recognition. The result of this is that lower probability features of the environment do not qualify for recognition because the classification process has been completed on the basis of the higher probability evidence.

Churches are the easiest building type with which to exemplify this situation since they usually have a powerful stylistic imprint. The first Gothic church to be encountered arouses full attention because of its novelty. Henceforth it becomes the datum of perception for other Gothic churches. The more of them that are experienced, the less they stimulate awareness. Eventually the mere tip of a Gothic spire suggests a schematic probability which causes full classification to occur within the memory schema, without reference to the complete building. This may be called 'system-maximization' – the method which the brain employs to streamline the whole business of perception. This extremely rapid method of classification by means of a minimum of cues has its advantages, particularly when an urgent response to an approaching hazard is required: a facility most frequently enjoyed by road users.

One useful ability arising from this characteristic is experienced in reading. A text can rapidly be assimilated because classification of words and even whole sentences can be achieved by recognizing the probability established by just a few letters. A number of psychological parlour tricks illustrate this capacity of the mind. However, this system-maximizing tendency has drawbacks. In achieving rapid classification, subtleties are lost and indeed whole sentences can be misperceived.

Under the rules of system-maximization, perception tends to be reduced to ultimate simplicity. It is progressively satisfied by data which yield to straight-forward categorization, and if the presentation does not entirely fit, certain adjustments may be made to suit the filing system. Subtleties are lost in the process. For example, a Georgian house may be perceived. In this country most people possess a Georgian house sub-schema which may be diagrammatically represented by a rectangle.

'Centring'

Georgian house
sub-schema

A particular Georgian house may coincide in many respects with the sub-schema, but not entirely.

'Centring'

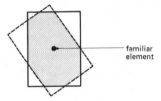

familiar
element

This facet of the brain tends to make the new object centre upon the established pattern, with a consequent distortion of detail.

'Centring'

In engram terms the situation may be represented in the manner shown.

37

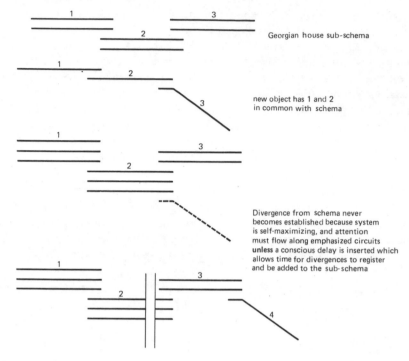

Georgian house (atypical)

When the mind is developing, this delay is often automatically inserted by the curiosity drive, so that the uniqueness of an object can be registered. Later in life, as patterns are more heavily emphasized, this has to be a conscious act of perceptiveness. Clichés can dominate perception as well as thought processes.

The same thing happens with words denoting an architectural style. In England a new phenomenon appeared in architecture in the fifties and was launched by architects Alison and Peter Smithson. It received the description 'Brutalism'. Very quickly this became a polarizing word – a category into which buildings were placed with a consequent fall-off in the fullness of perception of these buildings. The next stage was that the tail began to wag the dog and Brutalism became a style to be emulated. Now it is neatly filed away with other historic styles.

Perception may also be distorted by another role of dubious advantage which the brain performs: the facility to construct myths. This is perhaps more relevant to the design field than perception, but it is worthy of consideration. Myths are totally convincing patterns of unreality. In de Bono's terms they are 'patterns which exist on the special memory surface but not necessarily anywhere else', and they ultimately become a way of seeing the world.

In its dual capacity the brain first divides incoming data into appropriate attention units. The second, combining function reassembles the units into patterns, and where these patterns have been changed in order and shape during the process, the result is a myth. The great danger is that the myth becomes a preferable substitute for reality. By the rules of system-maximization the more the myth is entertained the more it becomes established as a mode of perception. Myths dominate creative fields such as architecture and planning. From the beginning of city civilization, the Utopians have been impelled onwards by varied and sometimes beautiful myths about the universe. In some ways they are like working hypotheses, but infinitely harder to modify or eradicate.

In the matter of perception, myths can be determinative. The principle of apartheid is an example of a widely shared myth rationalized into government policy. Similarly acculturated myths can influence an individual's response to a particular environmental array, especially with regard to symbolically-intensive objects like churches and Big Bens.

A final operational characteristic of the memory-recall system which is relevant to the perception of built environment concerns the effect of context. In engram notation, this means that a memory pattern might be activated in different ways according to the point of entry into the pattern. As discussed earlier, patterns are interconnected with inconceivable complexity, and the position of the adjacent pattern affording entry into the pattern in question is of great importance.

It is a commonplace to say that a visual event is coloured by its context. Dimensions and directions undergo apparent change according to the nature of their immediate environment.

Represented in engram notation, a memory pattern may be represented as follows:

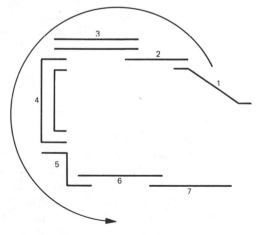

The arrow represents the normal way of perceiving the array

If a new building is inserted into the complex, with elements from a different cognitive schema, not only is the pattern changed, but so is the mode of perceiving the visual array.

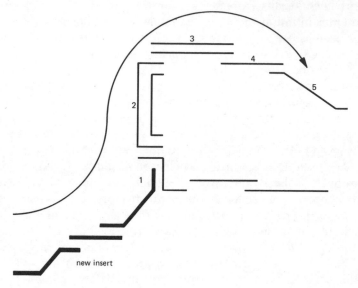

Engram flow probability

The new insert, by its novelty, is the starting-point of perception and so modifies perception of the whole gestalt.

'Reflexivity' is extremely significant in determining the style of perception. All the elements of the built milieu interact and any change has repercussions far beyond the boundaries of the new insert.

Relatedness in time as well as space can be affected by this perceptual characteristic. This will be familiar to all urban dwellers who have watched their town centres being redeveloped. New buildings are always evaluated in the light of the structures they replaced. By virtue of this brain characteristic, the bias tends to favour the latter. This could be described as the 'carry-over' from related patterns.

If system-maximization is allowed to go unchecked it can conceivably have an adverse effect upon the performance of the mind. There is only a fixed amount of energy available for the stimulation of memory patterns during the perceptual process. As patterns become increasingly deeply 'incised' so they dominate in the competition for attention. This means that the mind becomes progressively biased in favour of the familiar. As the more familiar patterns are increasingly maximized, so less familiar ones get progressively lower in probability.

This means that some material in storage becomes less and less available to recall as dominant patterns monopolize the system. So the ability to process novelty and the unfamiliar in the visual array, under the mechanical rules of the system, tends to weaken as experience is progressively confined to the familiar.

In terms of a graph this may be represented in the manner shown.

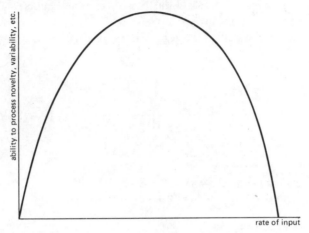

Novelty against input rate

However, this is not the entire picture. The memory-recall system seems to be a disciple of Darwinian selection. Patterns of memory are analogous to natural species. Strong patterns, because of this rule of positive feedback lowering the threshold of activation, become gradually stronger. Conversely, weaker patterns are victims of the rule of negative feedback.

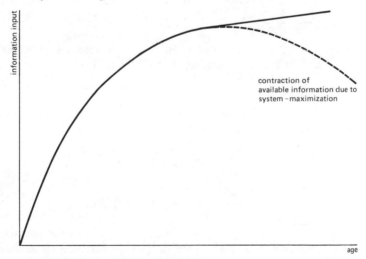

Contraction of pool of available information

Like weaker species they eventually become inaccessible to recall and so, for practical purposes, are extinct. So the matrix of memory contracts.

This is a sinister situation because it means that starvation in terms of varied perceptual events leads to a lowering in the performance of the mind. A negative momentum is set up whereby preference is given to a diminishing number of patterns which eventually tyrannize the system. The door to new experience and the formation of new schemas of memory is firmly closed. The mind regresses.

A pattern of memory may be represented by this engram figure:

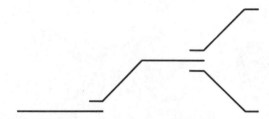

Part of this pattern becomes emphasized by repeated perception:

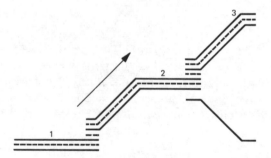

This now means that attention has an increased probability of following the emphasized route to the detriment of that part less 'incised'.

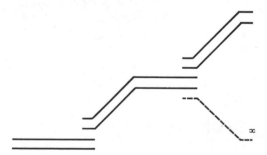

So element 'x' diminishes in probability until its chances of excitation virtually disappear.

When psychologists talk about the debilitating affects of urban monotony, they mean that it is not merely undesirable but positively harmful. It can impair the capacity not only to perceive but also to solve problems. Terms like 'concrete jungle' seem no longer appropriate because a jungle is full of interest and challenge. 'Concrete wilderness' would be better.

Returning to the semantic analogy, this abdication to high probability words and sentences results in a contraction of vocabulary. Furthermore, this means that fewer and fewer concepts become available to thought. The same rule applies to the vocabulary of urban events. Superficial identification on the basis of a few recognizable features frustrates perception of the rich variety of differences which may lie just below the surface of the obvious. Eventually the surface hardens and becomes impenetrable.

In Chapter 3 it was proposed that there are two major factors which can distort the operation of the mechanisms responsible for perception and evaluation. The first concerned characteristics of the memory-recall system, and demonstrated how there is a built-in tendency towards system-maximization: the progressive simplification of schemas.

This aspect has been considered at some length in the belief that it helps in the design process to know something about the mechanisms of perception. The brain, considered as a system, is the universal common factor, and it seems logical to begin by seeing if the physiological processes of perception have an influence upon the way in which buildings actually are seen.

The second major factor which can throw a bias into the process of perception is that wondrously complex and shifting equation known as personality. Before seeing how bias operates in this context, some words of general explanation are necessary.

By simple accretion, and by the interconnection of units of memory, a macroschema of urban events is gradually constructed. This forms the datum of cognition for all new, or at least partially new, urban experiences. The element of personality influences the mental *attitude* to data according to their relationship to the macroschema.

Before this point is elaborated it is necessary to propose cognitive categories denoting degrees of divergence from a macroschematic norm. There are no rigid boundaries here. Though the categories are generally applicable, what qualifies for a particular category is determined by experience and personality; so boundaries are infinitely variable. Even so, there is evidence that the ability to process variability, change and novelty is surprisingly constant among a large consensus of the population.[1]

So, whilst boundaries between categories are blurred, they are nevertheless discernable. When there is total affinity between external events and internal models, this perceptual experience may be called *schematic*. This is obviously the case where the environment is familiar and the mind has stopped picking up new events. The term can also be applied where sequences of buildings or individual pieces of architecture may superficially constitute a new experience. Nevertheless, they are easily perceived and responded to because all their constituent elements link up with material in storage. Though they are assembled in a unique manner, this is subordinate to the fact that the basic building-blocks are familiar. Such a building or array of buildings may be described as *schematic*, because all visual events and relationships correspond with stored data. Further classification of elements of the built environment is a question of divergence from the schematic norm.

The first degree of divergence shall be described as *neo-schematic*. In this category, visual events have a degree of novelty, but at the same time possess sufficient anchorage points to a sub-schema to facilitate cognition. Most new building falls into this category, though usually towards the schematic end of the spectrum. It is not a matter of architectural quality but correspondence between visual events and an internal model. Classification is a matter both of experience and personality. For many people a new Miesian-type office block might constitute a neo-schematic building. Others, with a wider architectural experience, would now classify it as schematic.

A building which is well within the neo-schematic category is the recent Crucible Theatre, Sheffield, by Renton, Howard and Wood. For the average city inhabitant there is much about it which is unfamiliar. Nevertheless it impinges sufficiently upon most urban schemas to receive this classification.

Crucible Theatre, Sheffield

Queen Elizabeth Concert Hall and Hayward Gallery

By now the same may be said of the Queen Elizabeth Concert Hall and Hayward Gallery. This is because of a degree of habituation and because the architectural aesthetic has now caught up with it. When it first appeared it was an example of the third degree of divergence from the normative schema. Borrowing a term from psychology which is appropriate, this group is called *pacer* building. The arrangement of visual events is such that it tends to fall just outside the normal limits of tolerance of novelty and surprise. It is building which disturbs because there is insufficient content to satisfy the demands of schematic classification.

Allocation to this category may be heavily influenced by other schemas. Earlier the example of the church sub-schema was cited. Certain churches may qualify for the pacer categorization in their own right and none more so than Le Corbusier's Chapel of Notre Dame du Haut, Ronchamp. Others like St Andrew's URC Church, Reading (GB) may be so designated because they symbolize a theology which is radical. The schemas have crossed-over.

Perhaps the most consistently pacer architect in Britain is James Stirling. His History Library at Cambridge still causes astonishment, as does his more recent residential unit for the Queen's College, Oxford, the Florey Building.

Finally there is a small category which is of relatively minor concern since it involves concepts totally outside the realm of the schema, and therefore hardly ever gets built. Being ultra-radical and totally unfamiliar, the title *a-schematic* seems appropriate. Examples of this kind of

Notre Dame du Haut, Ronchamp

United Reformed Church of St Andrew, London Road, Reading

46

History Library, Sidgwick Avenue, Cambridge

Florey Building, Queen's College, Oxford

47

phenomenon are not rare in theory. They are evident in the concept of the plug-in city, or cities built beneath megadomes providing total environmental control. Historically, the nearest thing to it is the architecture of Gaudi. Who knows what he might have achieved if his career had not been abruptly severed by a tramcar?

The Personality Factor

The organization of material in the memory is a mechanical affair, but the categorization is influenced by experience *and* personality. The personality factor has a good deal to do with deciding what is admitted to long-term memory, and can throw a powerful bias into the system. This next stage in the study of perception concerns the relationship between external visual events and the memory schema, and the individual's *attitude* to that relationship. This is what determines the like/dislike response.

Referring once again to personality theory, the spectrum is strung out between one pole which is ultra-conservative and another which is radical in terms of an appetite for novelty and surprise. Individuals contain both characteristics in different ratios. Also, a person's position within the spectrum is subject to short-term and permanent change for reasons stated earlier. Usually the permanent changes are in the direction of the conservative role. Imperceptibly the schema changes from being datum to canon.

The personality with the conservative bias has a psychological commitment to the principle of homeostasis. In mental terms this means that he desires maximum correspondence between external events and internal schemas or models. This reduces the task of mental processing to a minimum.

This commitment leads him to regard the normative schema as canonic. Evaluation is on the basis of conformity to the canon. Indeed it is possible for him to invest the familiar with a validity bordering on the sacred. He might be heard to describe a new building as sacrilege, and he means it.

Opposite in every way is the character with a very low cliché tolerance. He is bored with the current state of his schemas and is constantly endeavouring to extend them by means of new experiences. His bias is towards novelty on principle and he may not be too critical about quality. History and tradition are held in contempt as being inhibitors of progress. Of course the extremes are rarely represented. Everyone accommodates Apollo and Dionysius in different proportions, which is just as well.

If urbanism is to have dynamic potential, creative tension on the cognitive plane is an important contributor. Monotony is counteracted by buildings and urbanscape which are pacer or towards the pacer end of neo-schematic.

The tendency of planners in towns and cities is to eliminate pacer architecture in favour of the schematic and neo-schematic. The rule circumscribing design is 'fitness'. Innovation should not radically change the 'force system' of a given environmental set or milieu. On psychological as well as aesthetic grounds, this policy of good manners can be debilitating. While conforming to the Building Regulations and the Town and Country Planning Acts, it is difficult for architects to design anything which stimulates as much as a raised eyebrow.

In Britain and the United States, it is interesting to see how architects compensate for this circumscription, by design within the relatively free area of the universities. These organizations enjoy a degree of autonomy and wealth which permits them to give architects their head. In Britain this is particularly true of Oxford and Cambridge, both of which boast the most extraordinary recent architecture in the country.

6 Symbolism

Not only can objects be attributed with significance according to their conformity with schemas of memory, they can also be interpreted against a symbolic canon of meaning. This is a fearfully complicated and controversial subject and only a superficial discussion is possible within a general discourse of this kind. In this context objects are attributed with meaning for reasons which may have nothing to do with their cognitive significance.

Symbols are difficult to define, and dictionaries do little to help. The New English Dictionary describes a symbol as 'something that stands for, represents, or denotes something else'. More information is necessary if the significance of symbolism in built environment is to be appreciated.

A true symbol (as opposed to a sign) performs a function similar to a catalyst in a chemical reaction which enables two chemicals to interact without itself undergoing any change. Without the catalyst, the reaction would be impossible. Similarly, a symbol may bring the concious mind into contact with a hidden object or idea, sometimes liberating emotion.

Thus symbols are intermediary objects which have an attributed meaning. A symbol may be defined as an object (or sound, smell or texture) which imparts meaning to the brain, yet which does not necessarily bear a relationship to its phenomenology. It operates as a pointer to a level of meaning beyond itself. Probably the term 'vehicle' is also appropriate, because a symbol conveys attention to such residue of experience. Signpost into the past, key which gains access to deep-rooted memories, vehicle which conveys attention to otherwise inaccessible areas of memory – these are all valid analogies of a symbol, and contribute to its meaning.

Symbolism may link up with actual memories, but equally it may reinforce myths. Frequently, myths are the consequence of gross oversimplification. This is most regrettably apparent in racial attitudes, particularly in areas where ethnic polarities impinge on all aspects of life.

Quantifiably, symbols help to reduce the impact of impressions to manageable proportions, and this is what often results in myth and oversimplification. Cultural development in society, or the individual, involves the painful process of destroying symbols in order to reappraise the truth. This is valid in terms of attitude to architecture and planning, or religion, or anything which employs symbols. It might be argued that the British Monarchy has survived the democratizing process of recent years by itself being the first to break down obsolete symbolism clinging to its image. The Duke of Edinburgh usually manages to outpace the iconoclasts.

Symbolism implies system, even when that symbolism points to revolution. The symbolism of Montreal's Habitat was centred on the idea of a new order of living, but its datum for newness was the past. There is really no such thing as the present, only the future and degrees of the past. The present is as infinitesimal as Eliot's 'Still point of the turning circle'. The realities are history and hope, both of which are the currency of symbolism.

Certain symbolism communicates by analogy. Norberg-Schultz describes the essential characteristic of the symbolic analogy: 'Symbolisation means a representation of a state of affairs in another medium by means of *structural similarity*.'[1]

However, the correspondence must not merge into substitution. As Langer points out, 'symbols are not proxy for their objects, but are *vehicles for the conception* of objects'.[2] There can never be a point to point correspondence between a symbol and its object, though there may be a degree of configurative similarity.

An essential characteristic of a symbol is *economy*. It is a part which represents the whole. In the Middle Ages, it was believed that the symbol participated in the actual substance of the object. Thus a Gothic cathedral was not merely a representation of the New Jerusalem but was both an outpost and encapsulation of Zion. This was one aspect of the platonic philosophy which was determinative in bringing about the twelfth century renaissance.

Economy increases the impact of the confrontation between the subject and the image to which the symbol points. According to Martin Foss symbolism 'is exact the more it succeeds in omitting details and abstracting from everything which could distract from the one and only route to the whole. The tendency to exactitude is a tendency to abbreviation . . .'[3] A symbol of real significance has a poetic quality. By economy and compression it draws the mind to a level of perception concealed behind the normal presentations of environment. So, the most effective symbols are those which are imprecise, sparse and open-ended, tending more to the metaphor than the simile.

These symbols also have a certain paradoxical quality. As stated, there may be some points of correspondence between symbol and object. At the same time there must be a degree of polar contrast. In a sense the symbol has, in Koestler's term, a 'bisociative' quality. In so far as it is polarized with its object, the symbol is a source of energy – it generates a psychological spark analogous to an electrical circuit. Energy only flows if positive and negative poles are mechanically related. In the case of the symbol the poles are brought together to the point where there is an energy discharge across space. The most important symbols are those which release energy. This involves an arcing across the chasm of time, placing the individual for a moment in a stream of heightened awareness, perhaps akin to what contemporary campus philosophy calls 'cosmic consciousness'. In this sense a symbol can be a creative event; a catalyst which effects a creative interaction between hitherto unrelated patterns of memory. But this is the subject of the final section.

Finally, in this initial appraisal of the subject, many believe that there are depth symbols that mediate between the mind and ultimate images, and activate material in that area of non-conscious mentation which is shared by a whole culture, civilization or even the species. At this level, the impact of such symbolism is not undermined by the pedestrian processes of rational thought.

From the General to the Particular

There are at least four distinct fields of symbolism relevant to urban environment. They are:

1. Associational symbolism
2. Acculturated symbolism
3. Symbolism of the familiar
4. Archetypal symbolism

Associational Symbolism

Associational symbolism is of little significance to the architect, as it is usually outside his control. It concerns experience which is personal and linked with a particular type of environment. The writer once had the singular experience of being in an army truck which was struck by a train on a level crossing. Since then, level crossings have had a unique significance.

Possibly less traumatic is the associational symbolism of the place where childhood was spent – the home-town. Objects act as cues simply because they provided the environment during formative years of maximum awareness, or for the duration of a brief but profound experience. The style or value of the object has little relevance; what is important is the experience with which it is connected. The result is that successful people can become really nostalgic for the slums from which they escaped, often with great pain and effort.

Acculturated Symbolism

The second category of symbolism, that connected with cultural influences, is also associational. A different term has been used to distinguish the personal from the group association. Obviously, symbolism
of objects becomes more significant to the architect as its language communicates from the micro to the macro-culture. A Westmorland cottage
is a manifestation of a sub-culture and will have special meaning within
that locality. But its symbolic significance does not compare with that of
the Houses of Parliament. Having made the tactical error in 1940 of
diverting their bomber strength away from airfields to London, the
Germans might still have struck a severe psychological blow to the nation
if they had destroyed Big Ben. As a symbol which somehow compresses
the essence of Britishness, it is incomparable. Pugin did more for this
nation than he knew.

The Victorians were adept at applying symbolism to architecture.
When they built law courts, usually a heavy classicism was considered to
be appropriate, fusing the image of Roman justice with Greek reason.
St George's Hall, Liverpool, by Elmes, and the Supreme Court in
Washington set the symbolic pace on both sides of the Atlantic. Modern
courts like those at Manchester often communicate the same idea, suitably
up-dated.

On the other hand, civic leaders preferred to be associated with the
idealized Christianity of the middle ages. So monumental neo-gothic
structures like Manchester Town Hall inform all citizens that their
Councillors are always motivated by pure Christian principles, and con-
sumed by the desire to bring to reality the New Jerusalem. Such symbolism relies upon a common area of understanding within a culture. It is
able to communicate because people understand its imagery. They have
learnt the message by acculturation.

Symbolism of the Familiar

This may be subdivided first into that which is routine: the every-day
environment which forms a background to the day to day tasks. It is environment which falls squarely into the schema. Because it presents no
problems or surprises, it symbolizes security and continuity.

The other subdivision concerns historic buildings; namely, those buildings which authentically represent and therefore symbolize a different
age. It will be an age sufficiently remote to have been reduced to a symbolic myth. For Pugin the symbolic mythology of the middle ages was
dominant throughout his architectural career. For him it constituted a
golden age, and therefore this image interposed a psychological filter
which only admitted to perception those aspects of that era which
supported the myth.

One of the Etruscan Gates, Perugia

One importance of historic objects is that they place the individual in a much wider context than immediate reality. They symbolize the continuity of the mainstream of life. Preservation historically implies security prospectively. Human values, civilized precepts embodied in historic architecture, exert a timeless influence. It is not suggested that this is a rational response. The non-conscious mind is anything but rational. This is particularly evident when examining the symbolic complexion of historic objects. One characteristic of the psyche is that it always idealizes the past. This may be due to the mechanism whereby unpleasant memories tend to be suppressed, allowing more pleasant recollections to achieve a higher probability of recall. This gathers momentum as it passes from one generation to another, becoming increasingly collectivized. So in group memory there is invariably a golden age in which all needs were met and man was secure and innocent. Architecture can most easily symbolize this golden age. Greek architecture has led subsequent generations to idealize the golden age of Pericles. As mentioned, Pugin fell victim to the same syndrome in respect of Gothic architecture. To him it symbolized the perfect era when the Church ruled a society which was sincerely and monolithically Christian. The mind has no way of differentiating past time, and therefore all such symbolism tends to excite a nostalgia for the innocence and irresponsibility of the Garden of Eden, the Judeo-Christian golden age and humanity's womb. Such architecture sets in motion what might be called the Eden-chain-reaction. History is never dead whilst it lives in architecture. Buildings are tangible links with the past. To stand before the great Etruscan Gate at Perugia is to experience the full impact of history and at the same time fix firmly onto the Eden wave-length.

References

1 Norberg-Schultz, *Intentions in Architecture*, Allen and Unwin (1963), p. 57
2 Langer, *Philosophy in a New Key*, Oxford University Press (1951), p. 60
3 M. Foss, *Symbol and Metaphor in Human Experience*, Princetown University Press (1949)

7 Archetypal Symbols in the Urban Context

The final category of 'archetypal symbolism' is of such importance that it qualifies for more extended consideration. There is evidence for believing there is another dimension of symbolism which finds eloquent expression within the urban milieu. Stemming principally from C. G. Jung is the theory that certain symbols represent archetypal human situations, and such symbols have their roots deep in pre-history. Furthermore, their potency remains unimpaired even though they are now largely excluded from conscious consideration.

Because these symbols materialized at an early phylogenetic stage of the human species, they are collective, possibly even universal. They are referred to as 'archetypal' since they represent in objective form, 'the possibilities of typical fundamental experience such as human beings have had since the beginning of time. Their significance for us lies precisely in that primal experience which they represent and mediate.'[1]

In the opinion of Jung, these archetypal images have contemporary relevance and 'live on as systems of reaction and disposition which determine life in an invisible but all the more effective manner'.[2]

From the time of Jericho, through Sumer and the earliest cities to quite recent times the archetypal programme of symbols received its most elaborate expression in the shape and plan of the urban milieu. The question is whether this symbolic programme still has any validity. This can only be established if there is any force behind the hypothesis that ancient symbols do in fact live on as inchoate needs and systems of reaction to urban configurations.

External evidence to support the hypothesis is provided by the vast numbers that gravitate each year to the ancient towns and cities of Europe. The preponderance seems to be from the USA where urbanism most expresses values other than human. A German town like Rothenburg could, in the season, be taken for a transatlantic transplant somewhere in the mid-west. However, it is certain Italian towns which seem to be closest to the archetypal wavelength.

Certainly part of the reason for their popularity lies in their historicity. They are symbols of permanence in a world where so much is transient and high-speed. But their real importance lies in the possibility that somehow they generate a deep-rooted resonance along a time dimension represented within the historic development of the brain.

Increasingly the 'clean slate' or 'empty bucket' theory of human behaviour, which proposes that all human life starts with a completely virgin cortex, is receding in credibility. Evidence of engrammed circuits or templates being present at birth, which predetermine responses to environmental stimuli, is constantly expanding. One of the leaders in the field is Noam Chomsky who believes in 'deep structures' which contain the homologous rules of language. The complex rules of language are mastered by young children irrespective of intelligence or environmental advantage. Furthermore, there is evidence that normal children in all countries master very different languages at roughly the same age and by the same grammatical steps.

Spatial perception, too, seems to be more than just a matter of learning. Experiments like the 'verge test' imply that certain fundamental space perception rules are 'given', perhaps for security reasons.*

If there are 'deep structures' which pre-ordain perception of environment and language, then there can be no intrinsic reasons for denying the existence of deep structures which shape perception of a symbolic language.

Three things influence human perception of the environment. The first is experience and its memory correlates. Each individual possesses a unique schema of recorded events which modifies perception. Secondly, certain specific genetic factors may have a bearing upon perception. Thirdly, there are the rules of the cortical system responsible for perception and these are common to the species. It is the deterministic role of the second and third characteristics which is of immediate concern. Prior to explaining why this is so, it is necessary to describe a little more about the cortical system.

The human response to environment is complicated by the fact that the cortical system consists of a federation of three brains which, quite frequently, fail to co-exist in harmony. These three sub-systems, as proposed earlier, map the course of human evolution.

Recent neurophysiological studies reinforce the belief that visual perception is a matter which engages the brain at all levels. Earlier it was indicated that the limbic brain has its own optic system, with fully developed powers of perception capable of achieving 'complex discriminations'. What is most important here is that it perceives according to primitive rules. These criteria are very likely to include a pre-disposition to respond to configurations of space and light etc., which strike an archetypal chord.

* A series of articles in *New Scientist* devoted to developmental psychology offers impressive evidence in support of the view that quite sophisticated perceptual capabilities are present at birth, (*New Scientist*, **890–896** (1974)).

Because the primitive optic system 'sees' before the classical system, its mode of response can condition the conscious reaction of the neocortex. That is one reason why this subject is of great relevance to anyone involved in urban design.

Questions regarding the origin of archetypal symbolism can only receive speculative answers, but it certainly has something to do with man's infantile experiences as a new species. There are numerous hypotheses regarding the point at which primitive man was driven to cross the threshold to become *Genus Homo*. It is probable that the ability to objectivize environment was associated with this event. The capacity to stand outside the system of nature and observe it as something separate from 'self' must have been both exhilarating and traumatic. In the Jewish mythology the event seems to have been symbolized by the eating of forbidden fruit from the Tree of Knowledge. The awareness of nakedness is a good way of describing the first realization of objective truth.

With this realization came awareness of the ambivalence of nature as the agent both of life and, all too frequently, destruction. So, to compensate for his comparative impotence in the face of these forces, man created a range of symbols, or intermediary objects, designed to enhance his powers and enlist the support of the super-powers, the gods. Initially it seems that symbolism was the vehicle of human development. It enabled man to come to terms with his situation by creating artefacts upon which he could project his needs and ideal objects with which he could personally identify.

Evidence of this power of symbolization goes back at least 30 000 years judging by the reliefs in the Altamira caves. This means that the ability to use symbols was developed well within the regime of the palaeo-mammalian brain, and apparently before the full utilization of the reasoning potential of the neocortex.

Quite an elaborate repertoire of symbolism was developed at the predatory and nomadic stages of cultural development. But the great symbolic leap forward followed from the 'invention' of agriculture, necessitating a settled and heavily defended existence. This revolutionary change appears first to have been manifest in Jericho. In this prototype city, man first elevated and expanded the ancient programme of symbolism to the level of a whole urban artefact.

As urbanism developed in scale and sophistication to produce such miracles of achievement as the cities of Sumer, the symbolic programme likewise became more elaborate and all-embracing.

Rykwert describes how the inauguration of a city was a solemn religious occasion which had the effect of uniting the citizens with the universal order.[3] The city was conceived and planned as a diagram of the cosmos, and the diagram usually consisted of variations on the Mandala

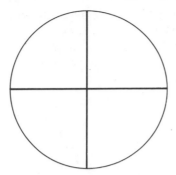

Mandala figure

theme. It is interesting to note that the Mandala figure turned out to be one of the most persistent archetypal themes to emerge from Jung's case studies. He became convinced that it was figuratively engrammed in the 'collective unconscious'.

Referring to the Sumerians, Sybil Moholy-Nagy believes that:

Their specific brand of urban piety consisted of the claim to have created a micro-cosm on a par with the galaxies. The construction of a Ziggurat . . . established a city-state at the dead centre of earth and sky . . . Man at the centre of the universe was not a geographical fact but a (philosophical) truth.[4]

Anthropologist and theologian Mircea Eliade believes the symbolism of Sumer had a much wider application:

Every oriental city was standing, in effect, at the centre of the World. Babylon, was Bab-ilani, a 'gate of the gods', for it was there that the gods came down to earth. The capital of the ideal Chinese Sovereign was situated . . . at the intersection of the three cosmic zones, Heaven, Earth and Hell.[5]

This is the heart of the matter of urban symbolism. For several thousands of years, it was believed that the city was the place where man came closest to the gods. It was the acknowledged meeting place accepted by the gods, the place of ultimate encounter. At the apex of the symbolic 'world mountain', the high priest enlisted the aid of the super-powers in support of the collective planning strategy. (Such a practice might be useful today. It would provide a rational explanation for some of the more bizarre planning decisions.)

Eliade concludes:

Every microcosm, every inhabited region has what may be called a 'centre'; that is to say a place that is sacred above all. It is there, in that centre, that the sacred manifests itself in its totality.[5]

This symbolic force transcended fundamental religious boundaries, as evidenced by the fact that the sacred platform of Jerusalem was assimil-ated into the Mohammedan world view without any problem. Indeed it was said to be the spot from which Mohammed himself ascended to God, aided on his way by his mysterious steed, al-Buraq, or 'Lightning'. Today we have Cape Kennedy.

Another variation on this archetypal theme was the World Tree or Sacred Pillar which has its roots or foundations in hell and reaches up to the corners of the universe.

Eliade maintains that:

Vedic India, ancient China and Germanic mythology as well as 'primitive' religions, all held different versions of this cosmic tree, whose branches reached to heaven.[5]

All of which provides a good explanation for the Tower of Babel. It also explains the symbolic motivation behind a great deal of subsequent architecture. The ancient idea of the Cosmic Tree was quickly adapted to Christian use and applied to the Cross, which a Byzantine liturgy describes as a tree which 'springing from the depths of the earth has risen to the centre of the earth . . . and sanctifies the Universe into its limits'.

This ancient heritage of symbolism reached its most sophisticated

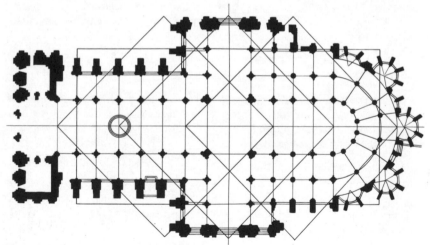

Plan of Cathedral of the Virgin, Chartres

architectural expression in the medieval cathedral. Chartres was constructed in every detail according to the mathematics of the universe contained in the sacred diagram. At the highest point of the ancient town, it comprised a cosmic mountain. The sacred pillars of its spires soared to the heavens. Beneath its high altar was concealed a primordial well which tradition regarded as penetrating to the nether regions. We are now left with the mere aesthetics of Chartres, which even so make it one of the most impressive buildings of all time. How much more must it have meant to the men of the thirteenth century. For a moment in

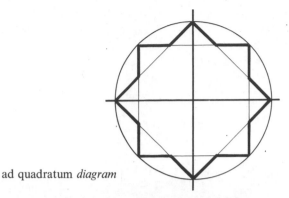

ad quadratum *diagram*

history it must have seemed that the long journey from the Garden of Eden to the City of Zion was over. The last of the great 'Centre' symbols are Liverpool Anglican Cathedral, built on a high outcrop of rock, dominating the city, and the nearby Catholic Metropolitan Cathedral, an almost literal interpretation of the 'word mountain'.

Roman Catholic Metropolitan Cathedral, Liverpool

Roman Catholic Metropolitan Cathedral, Liverpool

There may, after all, be some truth in the affirmation by Heinrich Zimmer, that

Ages and attitudes of man that are long gone by still survive in the deeper unconscious layers of the Soul [or in the deeper folds of the limbic brain]. The spiritual heritage of archaic man (the ritual and mythology that once visibly guided his conscious life) has vanished to a large extent from the surface of the tangible and conscious realm, yet survives and remains ever present in the subterranean layers of the unconscious.

Sacrifice

An archetypal theme of profound importance is the belief that life can only be realized in its fullest sense after an experience analogous to death. Liturgically this belief was acted-out in the rite of sacrifice which Dillistone believes 'is one of the most widely-practiced and diversely-interpreted religious activities in the history of mankind.' He sees a passive and an active component to this symbolic pattern.

On the one side there is the urge to accept death, to be immolated (symbolically) in order that the current of life may continue to flow; on the other side there is the urge to grasp life, to slay (symbolically) a victim in order that its life may be made available.[6]

Piazza del Campo, Siena

Religious buildings from gothic cathedrals to Hindu temples represent concrete expressions of the symbolism of sacrifice. In the middle ages in Europe there was no finite division between the cathedral and the city, which was equally an expression of religious pressures. So it is not surprising to find the tension between life and death extending to the dialogue between elements of the wider urban complex. Whether this is deliberate or simply the unconscious expression of a psychological climate is of little consequence. Especially in Italian towns, the dialogue between dark and constricted spaces and wide, sunlit piazzas must have a symbolic component. Likewise, when townscape which is sober in form, colour and texture is juxtaposed with architecture taken straight out of the Apocalypse, it comprises a dialectic which stirs the mind to the depths as much today as it must have done in the thirteenth century.

Tunnel from Via S. Martino to Piazza del Campo, Siena

'Canyon' approach to Piazza del Campo

Of all Italian cities, Siena is unrivalled in its capacity to communicate on this archetypal level. It has one of the finest central squares in Europe, the Piazza del Campo, culminating in the Palazzo Pubblico with its exquisite campanile dating from the thirteenth century. Yet this space receives no ceremonial prelude. It is encountered by a descent either through low, narrow arches, or deep 'canyons' through the encompassing buildings. Nowhere is there such eloquent expression of the theme that a symbolic death is a pre-requisite to ultimate life. To assume that this aspect of the planning of Siena was quite accidental is to underestimate the grip of religious symbolism on the medieval mind.

The same tension between the poles of existence can be experienced as one passes from an ordinary street of town houses finished in their rich golden-brown stucco into the cathedral square, dominated by the white marble façade of incredible complexity. It vibrates with symbolism of the eschatological city 'which has no need of sun or moon to shine upon it'.

65

Approach to the Cathedral, Siena

Façade of the Cathedral, Siena

Salzburg, Austria

Order

The complicated matrix of urban symbolism includes the image of order
being wrested from the chaos of nature. Man delighted in contrasting the
purity and sophistication of his artefacts against the arbitrariness of
nature, and none more so than the Greeks. Once again there is ambivalence present. On the one hand man enjoys subduing nature, on the
other he seeks to maintain his contact with it. His roots are in nature, and
he has no wish for these roots to be severed, just somewhat extended. For
this reason, there is great poignancy in the occasional solitary tree sur-
viving in a concrete jungle, which helps to account for the zeal with
which architects and planners inject trees into the urban complex. (Perhaps it is no coincidence that the author of *The Woodlanders* was also an
architect.)

The dialogue between artefact and nature becomes more intense the
larger become the values on both sides of the equation. Salzburg stands
up splendidly to the mountains; Chamonix is menaced by them.

Chamonix, France

Water

This subject warrants attention, for it is one of the most profound archetypal symbols. It is binary in its import, symbolizing both life and death. According to the Bible, the Koran, and Egyptian mythology, water was the environment from which the first life arose. It is the element associated with birth, and is essential to the survival of all living things. At the same time it is inimical to human life, and the cataclysmic evidence of this was the primordial flood. In Babylonian mythology, water was personified by the sinister goddess Ti-amat. One of the central themes of this culture was the cosmic struggle between the divine hero Marduk and Ti-amat, which Marduk eventually won. Similarly, the Mesopotamians nurtured the myth of 'the great combat between the god of the bright air and the god of the dark water'.[5] Sea monsters have always held a fascination for mankind from Leviathan and Behemoth to the Loch Ness monster.

It is understandable that in early religions, descent into water and total immersion symbolized death. Having been inundated in this manner, the neophyte would return to land resurrected and renewed, to begin the new life. The psychologist Erich Fromm describes the passages through or across water as 'an old and universally used symbol . . . of starting a new form of existence . . . of giving up one form of life for another.'[7]

So, when water was incorporated into the urban milieu, it was surrounded by a powerful symbolic aura. Even a fountain in a square, a pool, or a river had this profound binary symbolism. This was true of the impluvium in the aristocratic Roman dwelling, or the fountain in the atrium of the Christian basilica. On the larger scale, the confrontation between city and sea is of much more than picturesque significance. It is another of those elements which gives urban environment symbolic amplitude. Crossing a bridge, stepping up to the water's edge, these are experiences which still evoke a response deep in the mind, for they symbolize the essence of the human situation.

Image of Power

There is a final, important symbolic attribute of cities which has nothing to do with myths or magic. It is firmly anthropomorphic. One of the generic factors behind the foundation of the Sumerian city was the desire to project an image of power and superiority. The city expressed the corporate self-image; it is the super-artefact which wears the face of a particular kind of people, namely, those who press urbanism beyond the bounds of a town to that special miracle of commercial and political ecology and art – the city.

The Sumerians could never have come as far or achieved as much either spiritually or materially, had it not been for one very special psychological drive which motivated their behaviour and deeply coloured their way of life – the ambitious, competitive, aggressive and seemingly far from ethical drive for pre-eminence and prestige, for victory and success.[8]

For success in these drives the Sumerians looked to the gods, to whom they also felt obliged 'to fulfil the divine command against inactivity'. The Sumerians were a teleologically-orientated people, activist and compelled always to be on the move. It was not just coincidence that the Sumerians, besides inventing the city, also generated the kind of linear culture which has characterized the West ever since. For the city was the three-dimensional consequence of these internal drives. The symbolism and ecology of the city has been a prime driving force behind the meteoric 'progress' of western civilization since the decline of Sumer in the mid-second millennium B.C. Man has continued to create cities because not only are they tools for the shaping of collective ambitions, but they also symbolize the super-image of the community: they epitomize and idealize the culture of the polis. The entire Roman empire was a kind of radiation from the city at its centre. The Eternal City expressed the super-image of a whole nation which identified itself with it, and its impress was stamped upon every colony.

Identification

The motives which create a preference for urban as opposed to rural life may have altered in degree over the last four or five thousand years, but they have remained remarkably constant in essence. The present outcry against the dullness and anonymity of contemporary urban architecture may stem from the fact that society still considers a city should be an expression of its own super-image, and that image is falling short of the ideal. The citizen no longer wishes to be identified with it. This is important, for this indentification is something fundamental to the psychological support given by that city.

Historically, the symbolism of cities has been concerned with a complex mixture of commerce, politics and religion. The boundaries between them were blurred. Many of the opposites of life, such as the idea of two cultures, or the sacred and the secular, are relatively modern dichotomies. It seems that, until recently, men enjoyed being confronted with symbols of the polarities of existence. These polarities receive eloquent expression in the city which is at one moment shaded and constricted, and the next, spacious and sunlit. High-density, short-term dwellings crowded against the monumental architecture of the temple or cathedral. To walk through a city was to experience the pulse-beat of humanity itself.

Certain historic cities make a deep impact on the contemporary mind because they satisfy needs in a way which is almost totally absent from industrial and post-industrial towns and cities. The supreme contribution of the city on this level of need is that it can be a permanently valid symbol of the complete human situation – its tensions, its darkness and light. Above all it demonstrates the principle of creative, tensile co-existence. A town is sequential in its perceptual impact. Its strength lies in the principle of *relationship*, and as such it has almost a moral potential in countering the present movement towards fragmentation. The wholeness of a city can introject this principle into man as an individual and society as a whole. Perhaps the greatest need of the present is for the acceptance of the concept of unity out of diversity; enhancement out of tension. No other aspect of man's environment has more positive or detrimental potential in respect of this goal than the city. It is a responsibility too easily repressed by discrediting the problem.

References

1 J. Jacobi, *The Psychology of C. G. Jung*, Kegan Paul (1942)
2 C. G. Jung, *Seelenprobleme der Gegenwart*, Rascher & Co. (Zurich, 1931), p. 173
3 J. Rykwert, *The Idea of a Town*, an extract from *Forum*, published by G. van Saane, Hilversum, distributed in UK by St George's Gallery, London
4 S. Moholy-Nagy, *The Matrix of Man*, Pall Mall (1968), p. 44
5 M. Eliade, *Images and Symbols*, Harvill (1961)
6 F. W. Dillistone, *Christianity and Symbolism*, Collins (1955), p. 247
7 E. Fromm, *The Forgotten Language*, Grove Press (New York, 1972), p. 155
8 S. N. Kramer, *The Sumerians* (Chicago, 1965)

8 Relational Perception and Value Systems

Besides features which enable buildings to be categorized according to the schema of memory, there is a further system of perception which responds to the *relationship* between the elements of the visual array.

Whenever certain features show a consistency across time and space the result is a 'style'. Such a style is identifiable because it manifests a certain pattern of relationships. These may consist of the proportions of contrary dimensions such as height to breadth, the relationship between solid and void, the tempo of rhythm set up by architectural elements, or the relationship between materials and colours. A Cotswold cottage is as identifiable for its shape and material as a basque house with its deep eves and white and red ochre colour scheme.

These patterns of consistency tend to be perceived as value systems, and response to them usually has an aesthetic content. The term 'value system' calls for some elaboration. Even though there are diverse value systems in architecture and urban design, certain characteristics reverberate through all of them. An understanding of these principles is an essential element in the appreciation of the complexities of perception in the built milieu.

In the first place the principle of *relationship* is common to all value systems. A motif or object only has significance because it is related to other motifs or objects. A single note in music has no aesthetic potential. This only emerges when it is followed by a sequence of other notes to make tune, or is supported by other notes to make a chord. Relationship also modifies an object. This is plainly demonstrated by colours. A colour of fairly strong intensity appears to change its hue according to whatever colour is juxtaposed. The same fact is demonstrated by an illusion derived from two equal and parallel lines with contrasting terminal situations.

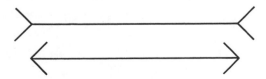

Mueller-Lyer illusion

Mere juxtaposition does not inevitably produce aesthetic potential. The aesthetic response occurs when attention fragments are combined within the brain to form a pattern which has both coherence and elegance. The element of surprise is an important but not essential contributor to this area of response. A *significant* relationship between parts is the invariable condition, and sudden perception of this meaning emerging out of a varied presentation of objects as figure against ground is perhaps analogous to a 'eureka' experience.

So the second characteristic of value systems is that the parts of a visual array cohere in a way which produces a whole which is of much greater significance than the mere sum of the parts. It is akin to the principle of 'holism' in nature.

At first glance, the variety of architectural style occurring across two millennia would seem to preclude the possibility of pattern. This might seem to be confirmed by two quotations which virtually mark the limits of the period in question. The first is a paraphrase by Alberti of the famous statement by Vitruvius:

Beauty consists in a rational intergration of the proportion of all the parts of a building, in such a way that every part has its fixed size and shape, and nothing could be added or taken away without destroying the harmony of the whole.[1]

The second is a recent credo by Robert Venturi:

I like complexity and contradiction in architecture . . . A valid architecture evokes many levels of meaning: its space and its elements become readable and workable in several ways at once . . . I like forms that are impure rather than 'pure', compromising rather than 'clean', distorted rather than 'straightforward', ambiguous rather than 'articulated', allusive rather than 'simple' . . .[2]

In one sense, architectural and urban development represents a continuum of change. At the same time, certain recurring patterns are discernable just below the cognitive surface. Development is both continuous and cyclic, and so is most aptly depicted by a helix.

The recurrent cultural cycle has three distinct stages, each stage representing a consistent and defined value system. Alternatively each could be described as an autonomous aesthetic.

The two quotations just cited mark the limits of a cycle. Though they seem contradictory at every point they nevertheless are organically related. Indeed this organic relationship could be conceived in the literal sense, since the quotations may be said to relate to the paradoxical mental drives present in every personality. One principle opts for equilibrium between inside and outside. In artistic terms it produces the Classic*

---

* Throughout this book the term 'Classic' is used to denote this cultural motivation. This is distinct from 'classic' in the sense of a perfect example of its kind. The architecture of Greece is referred to as 'Classical' and the styles of subsequent ages based on Greek architecture is defined as 'classical'.

tendency.[3] The other array of drives has the objective of optimum self-expression and realization. The constant shake up of stored information within the memory is high on the agenda. This is the radical side of the psyche, and in the cultural history sense is called the Romantic impetus; the aspect of mentation which is dominant in the Venturi type of personality.[3]

In Western society, the consensus situation has seemed to favour the second, activist facet since cultural change has been occurring with accelerating frequency. Maybe it goes back to the Sumerians. According to Sybil Moholy-Nagy 'this activist principle of Sumer formed the basis of future urban societies'.[4]

The first phase of the cycle may be described as the search and realization of a harmonic ideal. There has been no better definition of this ideal than Vitruvius's statement. This *harmonic* value system usually displays four characteristics, which are:

> Coherence
> Proportion
> Internal integration
> Cosmic integration

Coherence

The principal of formal coherence or wholeness is characteristic of all the classic eras: Greek, Roman, Medieval, Renaissance and twentieth century. This concept can apply to buildings or larger urban sequences. A coherent group of visual events comprises a visual gestalt or holon[5] which may be defined as an assembly of elements bound into a coherent whole by certain over-riding features such as rhythm and proportion. It can be detached from its context and analysed as an independent entity, and may be regarded as a semi-autonomous visual system.

A good parallel is a tune in a symphony. It is a musical period of heightened significance which has a high degree of internal balance and autonomy. Within a tune all tensions are resolved; the beginning is complimentary to the end, and the end is a logical extension of the beginning. Throughout this consideration of value systems in perception the term *relationship* will recur because it defines the core of the problem. In a Classic 'set' there is usually a complementary relationship between the constituent parts. As with a poetic stanza the end is complementary to the beginning.

A critical factor in determining 'wholeness' is scale. The visual holon must be capable of perception in a limited time. It must fall within certain psychological and cortical limitations. A determinant in the sphere of visual holon is the extent to which its perception involves eye and head movements. Beyond a certain point wholeness breaks down because it is undermined by the physical effort needed to effect perception. The cortical factor concerns memory. Once again an obvious example is provided by music. The viability of a tune depends on its length, because the beginning, middle and end must be perceived as a whole. If the end is too remote from the beginning, the form and structure break down because the beginning is forgotten.

The desire for wholeness and pattern is fundamental to the human psyche, and seems to stem from the right hemisphere of the neocortex. One of the principal motives in perception is the need to establish relationship and discover hidden patterns of meaning, perhaps because they imply that ultimately everything will be revealed as contributing to a cosmic coherence.

Proportion

The second element of the harmonic quartet is proportion. Theories are still being propounded about the significance of proportion in architecture, and sometimes the theory is the father of the fact. Maybe the desire to fit historical architecture into theoretical proportional systems is itself a clear manifestation of this pattern of psychological need.

Proportion is one aspect of the relationship between two or more entities which form part of the same visual system. Canonic systems of proportion, whether in a Greek temple or Ministry of Housing bulletins on Metric House Shells, are a manifestation of the Classic tendency to impose conformity: to iron-out individualism. Systems of proportion which have been more or less axiomatic tend to lay down relationships in which one entity exceeds the other by an amount sufficient to cause acceptable tension but not domination. In a complex system of such relationships, the various contrary accents would be balanced-out to produce harmony.

This is well illustrated by Greek architecture in which two basic proportional systems were employed. The first was generated by the ratio of one side of a square to its diagonal: $1:\sqrt{2}$ or $1:1\cdot414$. This was employed in the temples of Apollo, Epicurius and Zeus, Olympia. The second, sometimes described as the Golden Section, is more complicated: 'the ratio of the shorter side of a rectangle to the longer side shall be the same as the ratio of the longer side to the sum of the shorter and longer sides,' and produces the ratio $1 : 1\cdot618$.

In the middle ages one of the decisive proportional systems was derived from the pentatonic scale: $1 : 3 : 5 : 8$. These ratios dominate the design of Chartres. This is close to the Golden Section, and gets closer the further one progresses along the scale, for example $13 : 21 = 1 : 1\cdot615$.

Chartres interior

The unknown architect of Chartres seems to have integrated both the $1:\sqrt{2}$ and the $1:3:5:8$ ratios into his design. The plan yields convincingly to a system of squares. The basic figure consisted of a square superimposed on another square of the same dimensions and turned through 45° (see page 61). This figure occurs in several medieval drawings, for example a ground plan of a column base. It is also quite consistent with the statement that the cathedral was designed '*ad quadratum*'. This figure naturally produces the ratio $1:\sqrt{2}$.

The plan of Chartres also appears to conform to the $1:3:5:8$ system in the disposition of its main elements (page 60). Elevationally the whole interior reflects the pentatonic scale, even down to the size of the stones.[6] Altogether Chartres is the most astonishing monument to canonic architecture.

Since Pythagoras there has been a close relationship between proportional systems in architecture and intervals in music. It was he who discovered that musical consonances were determined by the ratios between small whole numbers. If two strings are made to vibrate under the same conditions, one being half the length of the other, the resulting relationship would be an octave, and could be represented by the ratio $1:2$. If the relationship between the strings is two to three the difference in pitch would produce a musical fifth, and three to four results in a fourth. Thus the Greek musical system which consisted basically of octaves, fifths and fourths could be expressed as the ratios (1 : 2) (2 : 3) (3 : 4) or simply 1 : 2 : 3 : 4. This progression also contains the two composite consonances of octave plus fifth 1 : 2 : 3, and two octaves 1 : 2 : 4.[7]

This relationship between music and architecture has been one of the principal determinants in design in classical, medieval and renaissance times. It reached its climax with Palladio in the sixteenth century. He integrated the complex musical theory of the time into his architecture with a consistency which is unique. It was all based on the principle stated by Alberti and derived from Pythagoras that:

the numbers by means of which the agreement of sounds affects our ears with delight, are the very same which please our eyes and our minds . . . . We shall, therefore, borrow all our rules for harmonic relations from the musicians to whom this sort of numbers is extremely well known.[8]

This point has been expanded to demonstrate firstly the fact that proportional systems have played a decisive role in shaping architecture, and secondly that such systems contain harmonious relationships which are most readily perceived through the medium of music. Also, the interval between numbers is such that the relationship is sufficient to be significant and pleasing, neither too minimal nor too great.

All this has been brought up to date by Le Corbusier. As with architects in other Classic eras he felt the need in the twenties to conform to a proportional system. The result was his 'Modulor' based on the ratio of a man standing to a man standing with arms extended. Happily the result was the ratio 1 : 1·618.

Internal Integration

This is the third product of the harmonic value system. During the Classic period of the Renaissance the ideal geometrical figure was the circle. It was the perfect symbol of God as it had neither beginning nor end. It was also the symbol of perfect tranquility containing no conflicting elements or abrupt junctions. The aim of Classic architecture in all eras has been to eliminate conflict between the constituents of the artefact and reduce to a minimum the contrast between diverse elements. Greek architecture has become the archetype of this philosophy. Reduced to its essence, a Greek temple is a rectangular room on a raised base and capped with a tiled pitch roof. Out of this raw material the Greeks created the most sophisticated piece of architectural sculpture ever conceived.

The two obviously diverse elements in a building are the walls and the roof. In the Greek temple the principal walls are displaced by peripteral columns which have the effect of admitting space into the building, thereby reconciling outside with interior. The walls are 'fixed' to the roof by means of a heavy entablature. This gives rise to the problem of how to reconcile the vertical with the horizontal. The austere but brilliant solution was the Doric capital, which also integrated the rotund and the rectangular. The shape of the echinus moulding was gradually refined until in the Parthenon it effected the most subtle transition from the horizontal to the vertical. Where line and rectangularity were dominant features of the building, a pure cylindrical form would be alien, and therefore a linear quality was imposed on the columns by means of fluting, which was related to the standard module of the building.

The next problem was to integrate the side with the front of the temple. One strong unifying element, of course, was the peripteral arcade of columns. But this did not solve the problem of relating the eaves cornice to the gable end. Now, the Greek pediment is taken for granted as a lynch-pin of Classical architecture, but really the device of creating a triangle out of the cornice by following the profile of the roof on the one hand and on the other the horizontal line of the entablature, represents a most sophisticated piece of integrative design invention.

It is significant that one of the principal factors, according to D. S. Robertson, contributing to the decline of Doric architecture was the problem of the corner of the entablature.[9] Triglyphs were placed centrally over the column, but on corners it was felt desirable that the triglyphs should meet. This posed an insoluble problem which, to the Greek mind, eroded the whole integrity of the design.

The devices which Ictinus and Callicrates employed in the Parthenon to correct optical distortion have left subsequent generations incredulous. No building since has been designed to induce such a total sense of harmony and order. It is a building which harmonizes with the natural phenomena such as gravity and light as well as the human demand for entire equilibrium. Subsequently many of the features of architecture which contribute to our understanding of style are extensions of that classical vocabulary designed to achieve harmonious integration between all contrary elements.

The next era of pure inventiveness was during the eleventh and twelfth centuries. Once again the equilibration of inferred forces was a principal design intention. Churches like the Abbey of Saint Madeleine, Vezelay and Saint Lazare, Autun, and of course Chartres (page 77) are supreme realizations of the same integrative intention. Vertical shafts and horizontal strings modulate the interiors so that height is reconciled to breadth and the horizontal plane to the vertical.

The unity of a Greek temple or a Gothic cathedral owes a great deal to rhythm. A constant interval between a recurring element such as a column is a strong influence for integration which can offset diversifying features. In a medieval church, different but related rhythms are super-

Abbey of Sainte Madeleine, Vezelay

imposed in main arcade, triforium and clerestory. The main arcade rhythm may reflect the vault rhythm or be twice the frequency, as in St Etienne, Caen. In all cases the result is an over-riding unity.

Perhaps the most fundamental reconciliation of opposites is that which is realized between artefact and nature. This was probably the motive behind the medieval and renaissance practice in palazzo design of building the ground floor in rusticated stone and then proceeding to ashlar on the upper floors. Palladio achieved a subtle transition from the rugged and arbitrary to the sophisticated in the design of the Palazzo Thiene, Vicenza. The ground floor is of dressed stone but with deeply incised joints, and the top floor dressed stone with thin line joints. As the building emerges above nature it becomes progressively crisp and un-natural. But at the same time it is an effort to meet nature half way – an exercise in inflexion.

Cathedral of Saint Lazare, Autun

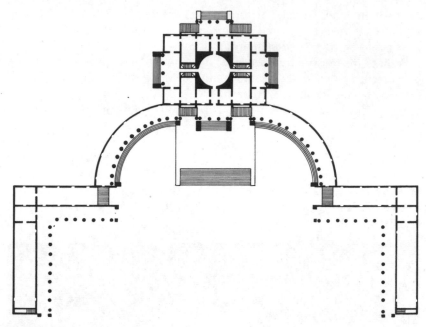

Villa Trissino, Meledo (plan)

The same architect achieved a different form of reconciliation between architecture and nature in his country villas, such as the Villa Trissino, Meledo. He devised the formula whereby the house extended two or four flanking arms which brought nature within the cutilage of the architecture. It was an harmonious partnership which made a great impact on the English aristocracy of the eighteenth century.

Cosmic Integration

This type of integration describes a need frequently expressed in art and architecture to relate the work to some wider order. Perhaps, since the development of the neocortex, man has required assurance that he is an organic part of the organization of the cosmos. This involvement of man in the macrocosm has been a preoccupation of philosophers, theologians, artists and architects since earliest times.

The link between man and the universe has most commonly been achieved through mathematics. At first this may appear to be a philosophical extension of proportional theory. There is a fundamental difference. Systems of proportion hitherto mentioned were evolved from harmonic considerations, such as the pleasure derived from musical intervals and harmonies being transposed into architecture. There was another strong motive behind proportional systems. That motive was contained in the theory that numbers embodied the mysteries of the world and the universe. Certain proportional systems have, from time to time, been employed for purely rational, philosophical and theological reasons. Plato must be accorded a good deal of the credit for this. Following Pythagoras, he affirmed that perfect harmony lay in squares and cubes, and that the integration of the two progressions $1:2:4:8$ and $1:3:9:27$ produced the secret rhythm of the universe. In *Timaeus* he conceived the primary bodies of which the world is composed as building materials . . .

ready to be put together by the builder's hand. This composition is effected by means of fixing the quantities in perfect geometrical proportions of cubes and squares . . . the same proportions that also determine the composition of the world-soul.

This train of thought was hooked-up to the Christian Biblical tradition by Augustine and his pupil Boethius. The link phrase was found in the Wisdom of Solomon: 'Thou hast ordered all things in measure, number and weight'. According to Émile Mâle, 'Augustine considered wisdom to be reflected in the numbers impressed on all things . . . the construction of a physical and moral world alike is based on Eternal numbers.'[10] These speculations were taken up and advanced, notably in three great centres of intellectual activity, the School of Chartres under Thierry and the monastic houses of Citeaux and Clairvaux ruled by St Bernard. Architecturally, the significance of this lies in the fact that the Abbot Suger, closely associated with Bernard, epitomized this philosophy in the design for his new abbey of St Denis. From then on mathematical mysticism was decisive in the design of buildings.

This has aesthetic significance in that it is all associated with the elegance of numbers. Man derived satisfaction from feeling involved in this elegance which pervades the universe to its limits. This was re-iterated in the Renaissance by Alberti, Francesco di Giorgio and Luca Paciolo, among others. Nor is this kind of thinking dead. The Cubist painters sought to convey a sense of unity between diverse objects based on geometrical proportions. The most architectonic of all twentieth-century painters, Piet Mondrian, was concerned with pure harmony. Harmonies perceived by the artist would gradually permeate society.

Then [he says] we shall no longer need paintings, for we shall live in the midst of art come to life . . . Today art is of the highest importance because, thanks to it, the laws of balance (harmony) can be directly visualized . . . Rising permanently above all suffering and joy is balance.

Compare this with Augustine and the idea that the construction of the moral world is based on eternal numbers, and it is evident that the philosophers of the 1920s, including Le Corbusier, were re-discovering ancient ideas of cosmic integration based on the laws of harmony.

It is no coincidence that this phase of the cycle warrants more detailed explanation than the others. A characteristic of all Classic periods is that ideas and canon are verbalized in great detail. This is the period of the cycle most heavily impregnated with philosophy, and philosophy must be articulated. So, there is more to write about.

References

1 R. Wittkower, *Architectural Principles in the Age of Humanism*, Tiranti (1952), p. 6
2 R. Venturi, 'Complexity and Contradiction in Architecture', *Perspects* (The Yale Architectural Journal), September/October (1965), 18
3 Ref. J. Barzun, *Classic, Romantic and Modern*, Secker and Warburg (1961)
4 S. Moholy-Nagy, *The Matrix of Man*, Pall Mall (1968)
5 A term used by Arthur Koestler to describe an entity which is both autonomous and yet integrated into a wider hierarchy. Ref. *The Ghost in the Machine*, Hutchinson (1967)
6 Otto von Simson, *The Gothic Cathedral*, Bollingen Foundation, New York (1956) and Routledge and Kegan Paul (1962)
7 R. Wittkower, *op. cit.*, p. 91
8 Alberti, *De re aedificatoria*, Book IX, Chapter 5
9 D. S. Robertson, *A Handbook of Greek and Roman Architecture* (2nd edition), Cambridge (1954)
10 É. Mâle, *The Gothic Image* (first published 1910), Fontana Library (1961)

9 Down with the System

'Perfection' can only be endured briefly. Utopia may be a heavenly ideal; as a long-term earthy reality its effects would be intolerable.

There are few who do not from time to time experience a desire to rebel against the social or political system, the prevailing order of things. Bureaucracy within the mind or society works on the principle of *canon*. In one respect the mind accepts canonic rule; it is glad to be part of a wider order and accepts the authority of its system of logic. This is Koestler's 'participatory tendency'. In this context clichés eventually dominate perception and thought.

The situation is saved for most people by a 'tiring factor' in the mind, something which generates impatience with canon and cliché. Iconoclasm is latent in the most conservative mind. This is an appropriate word because any bureaucracy gains power from the fact that rules which are accepted for long enough gather a sacred aura to themselves.

Rules take hold in architecture as everywhere else. This is particularly true in a 'classical' period (see footnote on page 74) such as the mid-eighteenth century. To deviate was to commit sacrilege. Yet how many in this so-called Augustan age must have wished to break free of the universal constraints? The few that did, Corneille, Racine, Blake, Wesley, etc., found life extremely hard. But the anti-cliché demand won the day with a torrent of bloodshed.

The fact is that the mind cannot for very long tolerate a situation devoid of all tension. Whereas one side of the mind searches out the rational harmonies of say Callicrates or Mozart, there is the other mental principle hungering for more abrasive stuff.

Anti-canonic architecture stimulates feeling because it overturns all the rules. It disregards the prevailing aesthetic, distorting proportions and undermining the whole existing system of visual logic. It arouses emotion more because of what it represents as well as its intrinsic relationships. At certain times the anti-canonic compulsion has become artistically transcendant, and is often first expressed in architecture.

If Chartres was one perfect synthesis of form with philosophy, it is significant that the formula was never repeated. Chartres was begun in 1194; the next great church to emerge from this intellectual maelstrom was Rheims, commenced in 1211. Stylistically there are many affinities,

Cathedral of Beauvais

86

but the impact of the internal space is entirely different. The plan yields to a modified Chartres system but the internal elevation is entirely different in its proportions. There is now a pronounced vertical attenuation; a deliberate move away from balance towards tension. Tension induces emotion, and from this point Gothic architecture sought increasingly to engender feeling rather than satisfy reason. Chartres is a monument to reason and balance; Rheims, and shortly after, Amiens, and then Beauvais, employed the same design vocabulary to induce emotions associated with the mystery and transcendance of God in contrast to the insignificance of man.

The deployment of architectural elements to stimulate feeling is a technique usually associated with Baroque, but always begins with an anti-canonic or mannerist revolt. Mannerism is a phenomenon normally connected with the Renaissance and particularly Michelangelo. However, it is the architectural consequence of a psychological change within society. All the indications are that man can only endure perfection for a short time; soon the habituation process erodes its impact, and the restless, tensile, exploratory, heretical side of human nature begins to exert itself. Artists and architects are usually among the first indicators of change. They become bored with the perfection they may have helped to create. Fifteen years after Bramante completed his perfect little Tempieto of S. Pietro in Montorio, Michelangelo designed the ante-chamber to the Laurenzian Library in Florence, which manifests all the characteristics of mannerism. Though quite a small room the vertical scale is dominant. Here is a space which induces unrest rather than repose. Its proportions are tensile, in that the vertical axis overwhelms the horizontal. All the rules of classicism are broken. In its day it must have been four-letter architecture.

The High Renaissance architects observed strict rules about the use of classical elements. Most of these Michelangelo reversed. Symptoms of revolt were present in his Medici Chapel in the church of S. Lorenzo, Florence, but the overall concept was balanced and disciplined. In the Library, half-columns, which normally are the strengthened section of the wall, are recessed into niches, reversing their role. To endorse the point, the architect placed decorative scrolls below the base within a recessed panel. This reversal of roles is most emphatic in corners where columns almost disappear. Wall niches display a total disregard for the stylistic discipline of the High Renaissance. Flanking pilasters have a reversed taper and 'rest' on a single triglyph. The capital is a constricted rather than expansive detail. Above the niches are panels of original design, and above these a cornice which is inset over columns. Here indeed, in the words of Miller, are 'tensions to keep us occupied and entertained'.

The most sophisticated and disciplined mannerist architect was Andrea Palladio. By no means as cavalier with detail as Michelangelo,

Ante-room to the Laurentian Library, Florence

Il Redentore, Venice. Interior

he induces tension by the relationship between the larger elements of a building. This is particularly evident in his church of Il Redentore, Venice. The design represents the most successful synthesis of basilican and centralized planning. The nave is a representation of a Roman basilica or great hall with three bays surmounted by groined vaults. The east end comprises three elements of a quatrefoil plan. The apse containing the altar consists of free-standing columns, the form being strongly drawn by the entablature. Beyond the altar is the Monks' Choir, a simply rectangular room, almost devoid of decoration. The result is a building in which three diverse elements are drawn together in a form of mutually enhancing tension. The three elements have a degree of autonomy, but at the same time they are integrated in a most stimulating and sophisticated manner. The ultimate tension occurs at the east end where the space is both contained and allowed to seep away into infinity through the Monks' Choir.[1]

The façade displays the same design skill. One of the problems which had taxed all previous architects beyond their limit was that of providing an authentic Classical solution to the standard basilican termination of high nave and low aisles, for which there was no Antique precedent. Alberti experimented with the Temple front and triumphal arch with limited success. Palladio conceived the perfect solution of integrating two temple fronts, one low and broad, the other high and narrow, both

S. Giorgio Maggiore

extremely distorted. The result is a wholly satisfactory composition, tensile yet completely resolved. Il Redentore manifests this solution discharged with extreme economy. An earlier stage in the evolution of this concept is to be seen in the façade of the nearby S. Giorgio Maggiore.

The impact of the interior has recently been totally undermined by an incredible piece of ecclesiastical vandalism. The building is now adorned with drapings and plywood baroque angels. The Monks' Choir is completely concealed behind a vulgar altar display which could not be more alien to the spirit of the Architect. To have seen the building in its original condition and, recently, in its depraved transformation is to experience a sense of tragedy. This was one of the greatest buildings of the Renaissance.

The next full-blooded mannerist phase began in the mid-twentieth century, and is still in evidence. Mannerism is concerned with reversing roles and undermining expectations. Recent architecture has exploited technology to contradict the familiar schema of structural and visual stability. Modern mannerism has affinity both to Palladio and Michelangelo in that it is concerned with major elements and detail. Perhaps the first indications were provided by Le Corbusier who launched the practice of raising buildings on stilts to free the ground area and lifting roofs clear of walls.

Erasmus Building, Queens' College, Cambridge

A building which illustrates modern mannerism is Sir Basil Spence's Erasmus Building at Queens' College, Cambridge. Mannerism opts for .tensile proportions in which the ratio between related elements shows much greater displacement than in classic periods, usually with a vertical emphasis. In this building there are slit windows uneasily related to more classically proportioned larger windows. A larger vertical slit window extends from roof to floor, without any reference to either. Another piece of mature mannerism is manifest in the separation between the stone facing and structural wall on the elevation projecting towards the river. It appears to float.

The History Library (see page 47) in the same University by James Stirling is no less mannerist. Here the context is a contributor to the tension; the building is visually linked with Casson's Arts Faculty complex. The main reading area is totally glazed and the junction between this cascade of glass and the L-shaped stacking block is one of the most polarized and abrupt in the whole development of architecture.

The mannerists are the people who keep a culture on the move. They question established criteria, and undermine the current *modus vivendi*. Perhaps mannerism is an inappropriate name, because it has a derogatory connotation associated with one who is mannered in his treatment of architectural decoration. The mannerist compulsion is something much more fundamental; it is the primary motive behind all human progress and endeavour. Without discontent in the prevailing ethos, civilization would quickly atrophy and die. In a BBC television series on the subject of 'Civilization' (later converted into a book of the same title), Lord Clark offered the opinion that Roman civilization welcomed the invasion of the first wave of barbarians to relieve the monotony of a stagnant culture.[2] The mannerists are the men who prevent stagnation. They assert the primacy of the individual over the groups. They place inventiveness before conformity and question even the most sacred canons and assumptions. They represent the prophetic vein of humanity and must include people such as Michelangelo, Ledoux, Stravinsky and Le Corbusier, to say nothing of Isaiah. Society often persecutes them, but it cannot do without them.

The anti-canonic phase in a culture lasts as long as the rules are remembered. Once they cease to register, tension is no longer possible and so the final turn of the cultural cycle brings in the phenomenon of the baroque. In the middle ages there was flamboyant Gothic and the extravaganzas of Henry VII's Chapel, Westminster, or St Anna, Annaburg, Saxony. The renaissance expired in the exuberances of Bavarian baroque. There is a complexity aesthetic in its own right which involves the enjoyment of maximum visual sensation. A baroque church like the Chapel to the Bishop's Residence at Würzburg aims to dominate perception, to overwhelm the senses by destroying the definition of space,

Chapel to the Bishop's Residence, Würzburg

concealing structure and creating illusions of light and space. It mesmerizes. This is a *polymorphic* value system, a term that describes multiform organisms and was lifted without permission from biology. It is used here to suggest coherent chaos. Psychologically, it is a value system which excites the limbic brain much more than the neocortex. The criteria of the two brains will be discussed later.

Rules are irrelevant on this phenomenal plane, and arousal is a matter of sheer density of interest. Each cycle expires in a frenzy of confusion. Yet the impetus behind a new search is already present. In musical terms the great chord which ends a cycle is 'enharmonic', having the facility of simultaneously ending one tune and beginning another. The search for an ideal begins all over again.

References

1 The interior as originally designed is illustrated in Wittkower, *Architectural Principles in the Age of Humanism*. Tiranti (1952), plates 42 and 43
2 Lord Clark, *Civilization*, BBC and John Murray, London (1969)

10 Value Systems in the Urban Context

The excursion into architectural history has been necessary to show that there are three recurrent value systems, each with its own hierarchy of rules concerning the relationship between visual events.

1a. Teleological phase – the search for a harmonic ideal, and
1b. Realization of the ideal – the Harmonic or Classic system.
2. Anti-canonic, tensile or iconoclastic system.
3. Polymorphic system; the recurrent manifestation of the baroque.

Value systems must not be confused with value judgements, and the object now is to relate these three value systems to the wider urban situations. It is important for all involved in the environment business, from designer to critic, to develop awareness of the visual potential behind all developmental situations, *across* boundaries of value systems. So now there will be a shift of emphasis from the architecture of individual buildings, to consideration of the wider urban milieu.

When one reduces the total built environment to its simplest concept, there are two primary situations delineated by buildings, the *static* and the *dynamic*. These are so obvious that they demand the minimum of elaboration. Static situations are those which, in terms of psychological forces, are centripetal. In Gordon Cullen's notation their emphasis is upon 'hereness'. They can be perceived as totalities. Dynamic situations are inductive, suggesting usually goal-orientated movement; 'thereness' predominates. Perception and evaluation are quite different depending on whether the environment is static or dynamic.

Static Environment

The elements comprising a static situation, such as a town square, may fall into a relationship which conforms to any of the three basic categories described above. Traditionally it has been the case that priority has tended to be given to perception of relational qualities from static positions. Town squares of medieval and renaissance times often comprise set pieces.

A static space in a city should be conceived as homogeneous work of art. It should qualify as an aesthetic gestalt or holon, a piece of visual lyricism amidst the more prosaic streets surrounding it. The term 'holon' describes in this context a system of visual events which combine into a unity which has a significance greatly in excess of the sum of the parts. A piece of urban 'poetry' can be detached and appreciated as an independent entity, yet it really only has meaning because it is an integral part of a wider hierarchy. It makes an impact because it is both autonomous and yet dependent on its context, a Janus quality which pervades the systems of nature as well as art.

In the contemporary situation there is much more relevance to the concept of *abstract* harmony. This is the situation in which apparently random relationships cohere into an arrangement which has an elegance that brings it into sharp focus as figure against the wider ground. It qualifies as art in the same way as an abstract painting, the harmony of a Kandinsky. Apparently random visual events suddenly cohere into a composition of apparent inevitability.

One of the supreme pleasures of visiting old towns lies in discovering hidden pieces of urban poetry. They have a pictorial quality which it is all too easy to denigrate in an age of rational processing. One of the greatest needs in new urban environment is to facilitate discovery of accidental 'holons of elegance'.

Anti-canonic System

The *tensile* value-system in the nodal urban situation is more difficult both to isolate and define. With the harmonic system the end is repose, with the tensile it is unrest. Tension is generated between the elements defining the space, and between the space itself and places beyond.

As regards the constituent elements, tension may derive from diversities of style. Here it is apposite to suggest that the tensile value-system is just as valid as the harmonic, yet it is rarely appreciated by development control planners. Harmony, conformity, etc., have their place, but there is also room in the built milieu for more strident stuff, capable of arousing feeling and even at times inducing shock. Good manners do not always make good environment. So tension between elements in terms of expression or style, scale, density, variety and amplitude of visual events is capable of aspiring towards its own particular visual apex.

Examples of this internal tension are too numerous and obvious to mention. Many Italian town squares will exemplify the other quality of tension between the place you are situated in and prospects that lie beyond that situation. The subtlety and variety of techniques used to achieve this form of psychological appeal is a subject qualifying for later treatment.

Finally, there is the nodal space which needs to be assessed by the criteria of the polymorphic aesthetic.

Irrespective of the position of the cultural cycle, there is at all times a psychological market for the experience of sensory saturation by a whole galaxy of visual events. This is the value of places like Piccadilly Circus. It is the focal point of a polymorphic maelstrom that has its own unique coherence. If the Circus is to be redeveloped, every attempt should be made to stay within this relational system, especially at night when electricity takes over.

Piccadilly Circus, London (Photograph by Peter Allerton)

Scooter contest, Cathedral Square, Todi

Unordered human activity has a vital role to play in this context. The mere presence of people in the mass is an important component of it. The importance is enhanced when there is an open-air market, or a festival or scooter race with a neighbouring town. .

When people take over the architecture, the result can have an appeal which seems to be undervalued in this age of overplan. It can be on the grand scale of the Palio of Siena or the intimate level of human 'interference' with a junction between streets (Via S. Francesco, Assisi).

Perhaps in the past the tensile and polymorphic systems of relationship have been satisfied more by accident than design. We should still create opportunities for these accidents to occur. Better still, we might give such happy accidents a helping hand.

Merchandise in Via S. Francesco, Assisi

Perception in Motion

Spaces experienced sequentially are fundamentally different in the way they stimulate perception. The analogy is between a painting and, say, a symphony or narrative poem. This means that relationships and concepts of wholeness are different. Rhythm and modulation are linked to movement and are dependent upon it for their existence.

Using the same three relational categories, the *Harmonic* system inspires relatively straightforward rhythmic relationships. An obvious example is a Georgian street in which there may be four integrated frequencies of visual events.

Georgian houses, Fitzroy Square, London

In the Georgian relational system, the highest frequency rhythm, which stamps unity over the whole built sequence, is established by the white reticular glazing bars and window surrounds. All differences of dimension and form succumb to this rhythm, even when they are as extreme as in the variations between houses in a sequence in Amsterdam.

The next highest frequency concerns windows themselves, which, in the Georgian aesthetic, or the Amsterdam style, are perceived as punctuation of the wall; they are the figure against brick or stucco ground. The next rhythmic interval is defined by the doorways. Being of lower frequency, they can be visually enriched and result in elegant fanlights, surrounds which are variations on the portico and the final flourish of a flamboyant brass doorknob.

Finally, whole blocks may be articulated merely by means of a gap, or more dramatically by linking arches in the manner of John Nash.

Tensile System in Motion

The tensile relational system would seem to have much potential within the current ethos. In the linear context it may be said to reinforce the dynamic aspect of the street, giving additional impetus to the movement compulsion intrinsic to it. This can be achieved in several ways.

Sequence of houses, Amsterdam

Palazzo (Galleria) Uffizi, Florence

Inducement to movement may be given by rhythm of high frequency. It is the frequency which provides the distinction with the harmonic system. The most pointed example which comes to mind is the Palazzo Uffizi in Florence which provides the two elevations to a street linking the Piazza Signoria with the embankment to the River Arno. Architecture piles up on either side. The rapid rhythm of columns at ground level, reflected in the windows of the three floors above, sets up a powerful directional emphasis towards the Tower of the Palazzo Signoria which is reinforced by four deep strings and cornices. This is inductive architecture '*par excellence*'. In a much lower key but also inductive is the rhythm of windows and cornices in an ordinary street in Florence: an emphasis

S. Croce, Florence

accentuated by the distant tower of S. Croce. This illustrates the further fact that tension can be induced by a dialogue between the immediate environment and a distant goal. Inducement to discovery is provided by the fragment of a potentially spectacular goal seen above roofs or round a corner; another aspect of the 'Hereness/Thereness' dialectic.

More subtle is the inference offered by a simple curve in a street, perhaps enhanced by upward contours; Trinity Street, Cambridge, is an example. A combination of these, an upward curving street with a fragment of richness seen from a distance, is part of the stock vocabulary of the more eloquent medieval towns.

Trinity Street, Cambridge

Finally, the polymorphic system has a place in this context. Perhaps this is the system with most immediate appeal, since it concerns visual events at about saturation intensity. The linear equivalent of Piccadilly is perhaps Soho, Carnaby Street, or the Munt Plein, Amsterdam.

View towards the Munt Plein, Amsterdam

Corner of Limburg

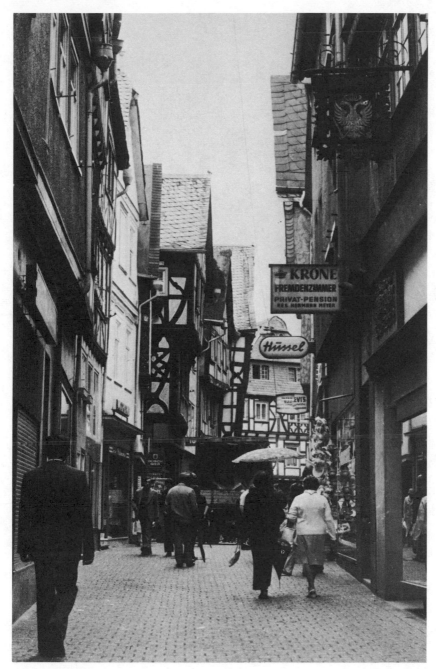

Street in Limburg

Street in Rothenburg

As with the static situation, this relational system is best expressed when human beings take over: streets with shops overflowing onto the pavement, cafe's that similarly encroach and take over pedestrian and even vehicle routes, itinerant vendors, and Seventh Day Adventists.

Many streets in the centres of ancient and modern cities make their appeal on this level, with a galaxy of advertisements, lights, colours, canopies, merchandise etc. In Limburg, Rothenburg or Salzburg the older streets fall into this value system with their variety of architectural events and elaborate signs beautifully executed in wrought iron. Take, for example, one splendid sign which certifies that the proprietor is a member of the ancient guild of photographers.

Assessment on this level has much to do with recognizing the transcendant coherence behind the inter-relation of parts. Good architecture and urban design is significant organization of elements to produce a new inevitability, an unprecedented elegance. Aesthetic appreciation is, in the last analysis, the recognition of a whole which is vastly greater than the mere sum of its components. On this basis a town has great potential to excite the mind by all three of the autonomous value systems, the *harmonic*, the *tensile* and the *polymorphic*.

Part Two
Policy

11 Design Motivation

Out of the description of the system of perception emerge a number of matters which have design implications, provided the architect or planner places human well-being at the top of the design agenda. The system of perception has been described at some length to indicate how certain needs stem from the very system itself. Until now, human beings have been considered in the design process as extensions of the 'self' of the architect or planner. Success in meeting human needs has depended upon the designer's capacity for objective self-analysis.

The attempt here is to bring human science more specifically into the design process and at the same time propose a design strategy which is human-centred. So now the focus shifts from description to motivation.

A design policy must begin from the understanding that the relationship between an individual and his town or city is literally organic. The unique configuration of visual events comprising a familiar town is represented within the brain by an equally unique pattern of cells and nerve pathways. Inside the mind is a permanent model of the town.

To stay alive, towns and cities must renew themselves, and this usually involves the demolition of obsolete property. Obsolete it may be to planners or shareholders. However, to the average inhabitant it may be a strong symbol of security, linking-up with personal experiences; a bit of the basic fabric of the complicated tapestry of collective human affairs. Often the replacement of familiar townscape involves a kind of mental surgery, the effects of which are rarely understood by those implementing changes.

Ideally the urban complex should facilitate, and indeed promote, psychological optimization. The Platonic programme for the city still resonates. The urban artefact makes its primary impact on the mind through the principle of *relationship*. What is more, it is a matter of *significant* relationship which in turn has much to do with rhythm. Towns and cities project rhythms on many levels, and these evoke a mental response. The 'rhythm demand' is a phenomenon known to psychologists and its importance is becoming increasingly acknowledged. Life is compounded of multi-layered rhythms, and mental needs display the same rhythmic pattern. The basic life-style is rhythmic and simple serial rhythms make a profound impact on the limbic brain. More complex rhythms contributing to order and pattern have a more cerebral appeal.

The city presents an opportunity to satisfy this rhythm-demand across a wide spectrum of individual and collective variability. Part One of this book described some of the rhythms intrinsic to urbanism. First of all there were rhythms generated by cognitive relationships, the schematic to neo-schematic to pacer. Whatever the like-dislike response to the schematic relationships within particular urban gestalten, their importance lies as much as anything in this principle of relationship.

Secondly, there were the rhythms apparent on the level of value-systems. The interaction between the harmonic tensile and polymorphic value systems was defined. Again one may have a preference, but the preference only emerges through relationship and rhythm. All value systems depend for their internal existence on this same principle.

Patterns can also register below the cognitive surface. Harmony can be communicated by a whole urban sequence composed of diverse elements, by overriding rhythms of glazing bars and window sizes, *vide* Amsterdam. It can register on the level of frequency, variety and amplitude of visual events. The more one learns to perceive urbanism, the more subtle become its rhythms and relationships.

Extremely important is the matter of symbolic rhythm as a contributor to the impact of a place. Here concern is with the rhythm between surface meaning and hidden image, between the reality and the ideal.

The urban system, in its pure phenomenology, epitomizes and magnifies human tensions and paradoxes. By its organization of style, space, light, constriction, gloom, order and apparent chaos, it represents a projection of the human situation. This situation can be exploited to the benefit of the mind and personality. It is of therapeutic importance that people should be able to project their internal situation upon external objects. By running in parallel with the complexities and tensions of the human condition, the city affords an object for empathy. More than this it can perform on its giant screen the drama of reconciliation. It symbolizes consensus psychological situations, overriding Freud's 'dialectic of neurosis' with the principle of *creative tension*.

All this constitutes a design challenge of monumental proportions. On the architectural and urban design side the challenge is to provide a rich variety of mind-enhancing situations. Saturation complexity, and exploitation of the universal fascination for labyrinths, deromanticized into the 'maze factor' by rational planners, are ingredients of the dynamic town. Variability, flexibility and multi-layered use, inference and stimulation of the curiosity drive, images and symbols setting alight the imagination, and drama sparking-off emotion – these are the stuff of pure urban therapy. They are being rediscovered now that the love affair with the motor vehicle is at last on the wane. Perhaps we can expect a new urban epoch in Britain since a Prime Minister had to abandon his car in a traffic jam in central London and walk.

It is also hoped that this plea will reach beyond those directly concerned in the environment business, to the wider educationalists right down to the level of the primary school. Edward de Bono has a unit in Cambridge which is researching into methods of including 'thinking' in the school curriculum.

Thought processes have always been taken for granted. It is to the credit of men like de Bono that we now appreciate that different strategies of thought are appropriate to different situations. If children are taught how to think both logically and creatively early enough, their problem-solving and creative capacity can be enormously enlarged.

Likewise we take perception for granted. It is regarded as an instinctive ability, which it certainly is not. Perception is taught under other names and covers most fields, but barely touches the phenomenology of urbanism. Children need to be taught the language of architecture and towns. This entails much more than the arid classification of styles which frequently passes for architectural history on school syllabuses. Towns and cities are Man's greatest artefact. They cry out to be understood.

If the preference for perception in depth as well as breadth is established during the formative years of childhood and adolescence, the mature person will never be content with a restricted diet of visual experience.

Despite resistance from some authorities, patterns of public participation in planning are becoming firmly established. People are demanding better environment. The art of perception, taught early enough, will ensure that these demands become articulate. In the last analysis, better built environment may only materialize because it is demanded by the participation of an *informed* public. Towns and cities can be lethal to the mind or they can stimulate the development of the whole personality, singular and collective. It really is time that we sided with Plato and opted for such stimulation.

12 City as Organism

As a preliminary to making more detailed suggestions about the ingredients of dynamic urbanism, it may be useful to establish a basis for a global urban-design strategy. In developing thoughts about the fundamentals of urbanism, ideas have been plundered from other disciplines in a manner devoid of academic morality.

Ever since a city was contrasted with a tree, it has been difficult to attract serious attention to the possibility of parallels between artefact and nature. So here is a challenge which most would be sensible enough to ignore.

Urban design is now a popular subject of study in its own right, and some attention is being directed towards discovering ground rules which can be universally applied. Maybe it is not too devious after all, to look to nature for guidance.

For example, certain refreshing ideas, which have interesting implications for the urban designer, are striking at the roots of orthodox evolutionary biology and genetics. A city may not be a tree, but possibly our basic approach to town design may benefit from adopting some of the design principles of nature.

The first principle which some claim to be universal is that of '*homologous design*'. In the biological sciences there is a rediscovery of the concept that the seemingly infinite variety in nature is not due to random mutations which survive through natural selection, but that this vast evolutionary tree narrows down through history to basic archetypes. The archetype contains all the rules of future development. They are strict rules inherent in the basic structure of living matter, which nevertheless allow scope for seemingly limitless variations: fixed rules and flexible strategies.

If the developmental sequence is traced towards its source it is discovered that only four chemical compounds constitute the programme of heredity throughout nature. If the four constituents are regarded as letters then each variation in nature is a different word. Nature is always synthesizing new words – continuous development in the context of strict homologous rules.

Can there be said to be an homology of towns? Are there core archetypal rules or precepts which are universally applicable? Certainly this was true historically. Elemental functions of the city were summed-up in the symbol of the Mandala (see pages 59 and 61). This figure, as mentioned earlier, dominated town design from prehistoric times to the Renaissance.

At least four cardinal ideas were symbolized by the Mandala. Firstly, it contained the concept of unity between man and the forces of the cosmos. Through the whole city, but especially at its sacred centre, men were tuned-in to the deities both above and below. A city created under the most favourable auspices promised the solicitude of the gods.

Whilst some would claim that such a powerful symbol-system must still resonate within the deeper layers of the non-conscious mind, others would regard the idea with scepticism. What is relevant is the fact that the town and city are physical means of integrating an individual into the much wider systems of nation, continent, etc. Modern communications give reality to the symbolism of a wider unity. A town or city is a nodal point in a complicated network of movement and being.

Secondly, the Mandala symbolized unity between men. In the city there was a social cohesion and unity of purpose which harnessed thought and effort to the common ideal. The city facilitated full exploitation of the 'participatory tendency', the need to give allegiance to a social group.

Thirdly, the two axes of the Mandala – the cardo and decumanus to the Romans – symbolized the reconciliation of all opposites. Transcending the diversity within an urban population was a unity conferred by citizenship. Differences were not ignored but accepted as contributing to the richness of the polis. All differentiation was contained by the bounding circle, which not only symbolized unity but infinity, having neither beginning nor end.

Fourthly, the Mandala expressed elegance. In ancient times this was associated with numerology, and thus the dimensions of the figure and the town derived from it were products of sacred numbers. In the Middle Ages all this was formalized into those compressed cities, the high Gothic cathedrals, which are the greatest monuments to this philosophy of sacred mathematics. The means may be obsolete but the end remains valid. Towns and cities need to be put together in a way that is poetic rather than prosaic. The greatest challenge to the designer in the urban environment is to impose an overriding elegance upon all the variegated ingredients of the town.

Historically, it was a relatively simple matter to conform to the rules of the urban symbol-system or homology. Today, urban problems have developed so explosively that the past seems to be irrelevant. However, nature develops adaptively within the context of environment, and the difference between the amoeba and man is no less than between, say, Orvieto and Tokyo. Yet man and the amoeba conform to the same homologous system based on the primary four chemical compounds.

To summarize: the four ancient principles of town design embodied in the archetypal Mandala may still be considered to offer a basic homology of towns:

1. integration into a wider system of being,
2. social cohesion,
3. reconciliation of all opposites and the transcendence of unity over diversity,
4. elegance.

Historically, the form and character of a city supported these requirements. They enabled a citizen to achieve a deeply symbolic relationship with his city. As this is the greatest age of urbanization, it must be a matter of top priority to rediscover how to establish harmony between man and his town. Maybe some of the answer lies in rediscovering archetypal rules, the homology of urbanism.

Stemming from this, there are certain global characteristics in nature which offer more specific lessons to the urban designer. In the study of genetics there is growing support for the belief that from the minutest living structures, the organelles, to the so-called autonomous organism, development is not prescribed by an imprinted working-drawing. Rather, cells divide and develop into subsystems which in turn differentiate into further subsystems by reacting in a particular encoded way to their environment. It is a variation on the theme of 'contingent optimization'.

This all means that the development of a complex organism like man is a matter of subsystems creating higher subsystems, and so on. The mature organism ends up as a hierarchical federation of subsystems (not really a contradiction) each with a degree of autonomy, and each contributing to the life of the higher subsystem of which it is an integral part.

This is the context in which Koestler coined the term 'holon' for a subsystem which faces two ways at once, part self-asserting and independent, and at the same time dependent for existence on a larger system.[1]

This parallels the psychological situation in which man is tensed between the desire for freedom and total self-expression, and the need to belong to something larger and greater than himself – the paradox of the self-assertive and the self-negating, participatory tendencies.

Two facts emerge from this proposition. The first is that nature comprises a vast network of subsystems or holons, each facing two ways – inwards and outwards. The second fact is that this network is not flat in profile but is pyramidal or hierarchical. The concept of the holon hierarchy in the context of an homologous canon of fixed rules affects the matter of town design.

Town planning is still heavily committed to the idea of zones of use. These may be in the form of concentric rings or specific areas. Zones of density also figure prominently, and it is not uncommon for these to be merely the consequence of lines drawn by a protractor. The zone principle is entirely contrary to the hierarchical build-up of subsystems which is characteristic of nature and, incidentally, many historic towns.

It is not being proposed here that we should copy nature for some philosophical or transcendental reason. What is being argued is that nature has a way of constructing organisms which maximizes the transaction between organism and environment. Maybe it is the tension between differentiation and integration which creates a dynamic which greatly contributes to the viability and efficiency of the whole organism.

Now emerges the question of what constitutes a subsystem in urban terms. The easy answer is to equate it with the neighbourhood. This does not suffice, since a neighbourhood is usually a purely residentially-orientated entity. A true urban holon should be a semi-autonomous and distinctive subsystem, possessing a good differentiation of internal function, residential, commercial, administrative, recreational etc. In fact it may be regarded as the town in microcosm.

Reference may again be made to laser photography in which laser beams replace the lens. The resultant 'picture' or hologram is an encoded version of the image which only becomes perceptible when viewed by laser light. If the plate is broken into fragments, even the smallest piece viewed in laser light reveals a recognizable version of the whole image. An urban fragment should have the same quality and contain elements of the broader holon to which it contributes.

The plan for Milton Keynes may have potential in this respect. Villages in the area are being assimilated into the city as developed sub-centres. This may enable the city to escape many of the criticisms which have been levelled against existing new towns, monotony being the chief complaint. The New Town of south-east Lancashire, centring upon Chorley, could also meet this requirement, though the existing sub-centres are distinctly lacking in environmental quality. Much will depend upon tactical design.

Where these two new cities may be deficient is in respect to the second characteristic of nature: hierarchical arrangement of holons. People endeavour to impose upon towns this kind of structure on a social level. It follows that a city will be infinitely more satisfying to experience if, in its basic form, it reflects the principles of the holon and the hierarchy. The holon build-up begins with the family, which is a subsystem within, say, a street, which is a subsystem within a sub-town which is a subunit of a city. The hierarchical climax is adequately expressed spatially and architecturally in the centre. Maybe the gods no longer meet up with the citizens in their particular urban centre of the universe, but the need for an urban climax which comprises intensified and elevated urban forms and spaces is needed as much now as ever it was as far back as Sumer.

The developmental strategy of nature has a further characteristic of value to the urban designer. The science of genetics is revealing the remarkable adaptability of genes. It has been demonstrated that even though nature is grounded in strict rules it can adopt flexible strategies under abnormal conditions. Organisms have the capacity to adapt to changes in both the external and internal environments, without guidance from any previous experiences. Several experiments have been conducted to show that animals are not restricted in their behavioural strategies to instinctive patterns but can be highly inventive when faced with the unpredictable. What is perhaps even more remarkable is the case of the fruit flies, which, by means of genetic engineering, were rendered eyeless. These sightless flies, who lacked the gene specifying eye formation, were inbred. Initially eyeless flies were born, but in quite a short time, sighted flies appeared. Within the genetic system there seems to be a self-repair mechanism which counteracts the deleterious effects of mutant genes or interference from scientists. In other words, there is a kind of dynamism to the coherent pattern of subsystems that enables the momentum of life to be sustained against the odds.

This digression into biology has relevance because towns and cities are constantly undergoing mutation. Evidence abounds to show that such urban mutations can be either beneficial or extremely harmful to the life of the whole urban system. However, if such development or mutation is closely related to an existing arrangement of urban subsystems, the momentum of coherence within the subsystem of urban totality will be sufficient to enable the developmental mutation to be assimilated to produce an evolved 'organism'.

This way a town or city evolves in response to developmental pressures. The rate of evolution may need to be fast to meet modern demands. New predictive techniques should be up to the challenge of generating change within the agenda of the rules of holon and hierarchy.

Arthur Koestler describes how the viability and strength of natural organisms lies in the tension and balance between canonic rules and flexible strategies which he calls '. . . the preservation of certain basic archetypal designs through all changes combined with the striving towards their optimal realization in response to adaptive pressures.'[2]

This makes good sense in urban design. The quality of many historic towns is attributable to the fact that they developed in response to 'adaptive pressures' on the principle of contingent optimization. They were conceived in an age in which change could keep pace with external pressures. Unfortunately when the force of these pressures reached explosive dimensions in the nineteenth and twentieth centuries, their adaptive capacity was drastically exceeded. As a result they either ossified into museum pieces or became entombed within modern fast-moving cities like Geneva.

All this cuts right across a number of current principles, especially the concept of zoning. The health expectancy of a town is vastly increased if its subsystems contain within themselves the potential to change and evolve according to varying environmental conditions. Jane Jacobs is absolutely right to affirm that the health of an urban system is related to its ability to renew itself to meet changing circumstances. In nature, the healthier organisms are those which have highly efficient adaptive mechanisms, like weeds and man! Design by subsystem hierarchy can accommodate change much better than design by zone of use or density.

Of course in all this there is no blueprint for the urban designer. Those who venture into the theoretical side of the environment business are constantly being asked for tools to streamline the job of tactical design. Urban design is much too complex to yield to design by tools, but what is important is that the global strategy of design should be right. The fact that the developed systems and subsystems of nature are able to cope with external pressures and adapt to changes, even catastrophic changes introduced by man, suggests that it employs a structural system which has much to recommend it. The design structure of nature consists of the principle of hierarchy comprising semi-autonomous holons, all possessing the capacity to develop and change, consistent, as Goethe says, with 'inherent rightness and necessity'.

Applied to contemporary situations, this strategic policy could transform built environment both in new towns and redevelopment areas. There is no reason why we should not cash-in on the craftiness of nature. Take, for example, the tree.

References

1 A. Koestler, *The Ghost in the Machine*, Hutchinson (1967)
2 A. Koestler, *op. cit.* p. 169

13 A Case for Challenge

It is now time to descend to the level of the pavement. In Part One the description of the system of perception included reference to two problems inherent in the system. The first concerned subliminal perception and suggested how the mental equivalent of the homeostatic principle desires maximum correspondence between external phenomena and internal models. In this way perception and behaviour can take place with minimum awareness, leaving response and executive control to the primitive perceptual system. Under these circumstances response may be conditioned by primitive criteria.

The second problem emerged as a consequence of system-maximization, the tendency of memory patterns to achieve a lower threshold of activation according to the frequency of recall. Thus the familiar increasingly becomes dominant in the competition for attention, and stands out as figure against the less frequently activated ground.

These are reasons for suggesting that a limited diet of visual events is not merely undesirable but results in a lowering of mental performance. Under this heading of POLICY it seems appropriate to reinforce this argument with evidence from psychologists, especially from the United States.

A classic experiment which demonstrated the effects of sensory deprivation was conducted at the McGill University College.[1] Volunteers were offered twenty dollars a day to submit to the total inhibition of all receptors. They had to lie on a bed wearing translucent goggles, gloves and cardboard cuffs. The only sound was a regular hum which masked any auditory intrusion. The experimentors were surprised at the swiftness of reaction. After a few hours subjects experienced extreme discomfort and later vivid hallucinations as internal compensation for sensory deprivation.

This is an extreme situation which produces extreme results. However, monotony can operate to the detriment of the individual over a long period and without being consciously perceived. Hebb claims that 'perceptual restriction in infancy certainly produces a low level of intelligence'. Evidence to support this claim is offered by experiments with rats. Krech, Rosenzweig and Bennett set out to discover if different kinds of environment have a measureable effect upon the brains of the subjects. Three groups of carefully matched rats were selected. One group was placed in a visually enriched environment, another in an average setting, and the third in a visually impoverished situation. Those from the first group gradually outstripped the others in problem-solving and learning ability. There was also a significant positive difference in brain weight between the first and third groups. This was cited as an *a fortiori* argument in relation to humans.

The deduction from this is that sensory deprivation inhibits development. As Parr comments: 'There has so far been nothing to suggest that urban monotony and experimental monotony should differ in anything but degree.' For an individual to achieve his full mental potential he needs to be confronted with environmental situations which challenge, disturb and enlarge his entire cosmic schema. The visual contribution to this psychological programme of development seems to be one of the most crucial, especially if certain writers are correct in attributing some social problems to the shortcomings of the built environment.

Woodburn Heron conducted experiments in which he exposed his subjects to a pattern of complete monotony. He found that the subjects became 'markedly irritable' and developed 'childish emotional responses'. There is no doubt in the minds of B. V. Doshi and Christopher Alexander who claim that 'mass-produced, mass design-regimented houses and offices stunt (man's) spiritual and aesthetic development and eventually destroy his mental well-being'.

Heron discovered that 'the higher organisms actively avoid a completely monotonous environment'. The most tedious road in Britain is the M1. There is a speed limit of 70 mph. Towards the end of a long motorway journey it is practically impossible to observe the speed limit. In order that the mind should stay alert, speeds of 80 to 90 mph are necessary. Only at such speeds is the rate of perceptual input sufficient to avoid debilitating monotony. It could be argued that it is more hazardous to observe the speed limit and risk the mind compensating by dreams and illusions. No doubt it will be a considerable time before legislators relate speed limits to environmental interest.

Parr relates monotony to social problems:

As we make our cities more and more uniform by design and regulations, we rob exploration of its rewards, till we force the young to seek the stimulus of the unexpected in their own unpredictable behaviour rather than in a too predictable milieu. On the basis of this reasoning I have already postulated elsewhere that there may quite possibly be some contributory positive connection between modern architecture and juvenile delinquency.[2]

Roul Tunley, after numerous interviews, 'found wide agreement that a thirst for adventure, rather than a basically antisocial attitude, is at the bottom of most delinquent behaviour'.[3] He then speculates 'how many of our restless, energetic pioneer heroes would have been juvenile delinquents if compelled to live today in our towns and cities'.

After presenting 617 college students with a random succession of visual forms and language sequences, ranging from simple to complex, Mansinger and Kessen drew three conclusions:

1. that everyone prefers a certain degree of complexity and ambiguity, as opposed to simplicity;

2. the degree of ambiguity which is tolerable relates directly to previous experience;

3. that through regular exposure to ambiguous stimuli, progressively greater complexity and ambiguity are preferred. This supports the belief that a rich environment produces positive feedback. This experiment may be qualified by the fact that college students were the subjects and they would be expected to be strong in curiosity drives and problem-solving ability.

In a further related experiment, Berlyne exposed his subjects to a range of visual compositions in two sets. The first set varied in complexity, measured by the number of distinguishable parts. The second set varied in redundancy of forms. In information theory redundancy increases with symmetry and predictability. In this experiment the objects were tachistoscopically projected for 0·14 seconds. But by operating a lever the subject could repeat the exposure. The result was that subjects chose to spend time studying the complex objects, but allocated much less time to redundant objects. As both time and complexity were measured, and the subjects had complete freedom in the time dimension, Berlyne claims that the experiment proves a conclusive preference for stimuli which involve a degree of open-endedness and problem-solving.

All this information seems to produce a precipitate of truth. A degree of complexity and ambiguity within the environmental milieu is not merely desirable but essential for mental wellbeing. It is the conclusion of H. F. Searles that the development of the individual personality is 'inextricably a part of . . . a matrix comprised not only of other human beings but . . . of predominantly non-human elements – trees, clouds, stars, landscapes, buildings and so on, *ad infinitum*';[4] in other words, a rich visual milieu.

If an individual is not to regress mentally, he must be confronted at regular intervals with objects and ideas which challenge his schema of experience. The challenge comes from things which are ambiguous, complex and open-ended. The maximum amount of this material which an individual can process before the natural defences start to operate is called his 'ideal'. In the opinion of Streufert and Schroder the optimum acceptance rate of variability and change lies within a comparatively narrow band of variation in persons generally. This collective 'ideal' they have termed the 'consensus point'.[5]

If an individual was never confronted with phenomena which exceeded his particular ideal or optimum perceptual rate, the ideal itself would decline. Habituation would cause the optimum perceptual rate to fall and negative feedback rules would apply.

The developing personality is one in whom the ideal is being extended to cope with greater surprise and unfamiliarity. For this to be possible, there must be regular exposure to phenomena which extend far beyond the schema and cause acute tension. Reference was made earlier to 'pacers'. These are objects or concepts sufficiently unfamiliar to lie beyond the ideal, yet not beyond the absolute limit of acceptable change. Periodic confrontation with pacers causes the ideal to extend and develop until eventually the original pacer level becomes the ideal, and so on – a positive feedback situation exists.

What is true for the individual is equally valid for the community. Pacers may be painful, but it is the pain of growth, without which man in psychological terms would perish.

This has been a brief sample of the mounting evidence which is being offered by psychologists supporting the view that built environment is a crucial factor in the expansion or diminution of the human personality. In the first of a series of Reith Lectures broadcast by the BBC, Frank Fraser Darling added his weight to the view that the visual barrenness of modern architecture is positively inimical to human welfare. Even the more insensitive are being rendered less successful human beings by the visual deprivation of modern urban environment. Thus it is not simply that architects and urban designers are failing to grasp opportunities, they are creating a situation which is distinctly damaging.

Parr sees 'a strong suggestion of important cause and effect relationships between our perceptual environment and our mental development, our rational or senseless responses in general, and our total personalities'.[6]

These psychologists can all take comfort when an eminent architect such as Robert Venturi claims to 'like complexity and contradiction in architecture . . .'

References

1 This case was first defined by Donald Hebb in the *Journal of the American Institute of Planners*, July (1967)
2 A. E. Parr, 'City and Psyche', *Yale Review*, (Autumn 1965), 76
3 A. E. Parr, *op. cit.*
4 A. E. Parr, *op. cit.* 82
5 Streufert and Schroder, 'Conceptual structure, environmental complexity and task performance', *Journal of Experimental Research in Personality*, **1** (1965), 132–7
6 A. E. Parr, *op. cit.* 83

14 The Dynamic Agenda

In Part One there was a description of the four levels upon which the mind perceives urban environment. Now in the context of policy it is necessary to develop from this level of analysis to the broader milieu comprising the medley of architectural sequences and complexity of spaces. The proposition is for an environment which, to return to G. A. Miller, provides 'tensions to keep us occupied and entertained', and 'surprise' to contribute 'to mental health and growth'; this is what is summed-up as dynamic urbanism, which, in an almost literal sense, means applying a force to the mind. This force causes the mind to react positively to external stimuli, either by formulating a motor strategy in an effort to satisfy curiosity drives, or solve problems posed by the milieu, or create images of possibilities latent in fragmentary disclosures. Altogether it is all about environment which stimulates arousal by challenge or novelty. For this reason the urban dynamic agenda is considered to be a prophylaxis for the malign aspects of system-maximization and subliminal perception.

The ingredients of dynamic urban situations are too abundant to enumerate comprehensively. Merely as an indication of the potential behind the subject, a number of the most obvious kinds of such urban visual systems will be described.

Ambiguous Space

Most spaces communicate two or more ideas simultaneously and so could be defined as 'ambiguous'. The term is used to denote urban space which is dynamically ambiguous, which means that it offers visual cues that other spaces exist in close relationship to it. The dynamic content lies in the capacity to activate curiousity drives, inferring a host of possibilities.

This quality of ambiguity or inference is well illustrated by the configuration of the central areas of several Italian towns. This particular spatial arrangement occurs so often that it might almost be described as a formula comprising two articulated squares. They are interdependent and yet each has a clear identity. Like the holon they are semi-autonomous and simultaneously part of a greater organism. The most celebrated example is the Piazza of St Mark's, Venice.

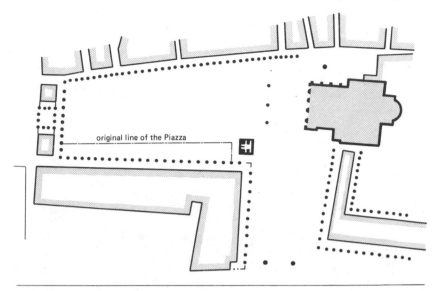

Plan, Piazza S. Marco, Venice

Piazza S. Marco

Detail, Piazza S. Marco

The lines of the formula were laid down somewhere about the ninth century A.D. To a large extent the cathedral square is self-contained. But the buildings do not confine attention to the space alone. At the eastern extremity a fragment of different architecture is visible. The exotic gothic of the Doge's Palace indicates that there is another space to be investigated. Upon this arrangement hinges much of the appeal of the piazza. This spatial quality is the outcome of historic optimization. The space was first modified by lengthening the piazza, and then later by moving the entire south façade to free the great campanile. The west

Piazetta, off Piazza S. Marco

front of S. Marco is a magnificent climax to the piazza. But that hint of the Doge's Palace is the prelude to another space of unique character. This materializes as an open-ended piazetta, receiving focal emphasis from two strategically-placed columns, and divergent emphasis from the view to the lagoon and the distant architecture of S. Giorgio Maggiore. Bellini's painting 'Procession in the Piazza of S. Marco' (Galleria Accademia) shows the square before the south side was moved, freeing the campanile.

The formula is repeated in the small hill town of Todi in Umbria. The main square contains the cathedral and Town Hall at opposite ends. Adjacent to the Town Hall is a break in the enclosure which draws attention to another square at right angles. It is a smaller piazza with a central statue, opening out quite dramatically to the Umbrian Hills. The main square evokes a strong feeling of *this* place, but the narrow break in the corner infers another situation – *that* place. Both squares are flanked by continuous sequences of building which would rarely qualify

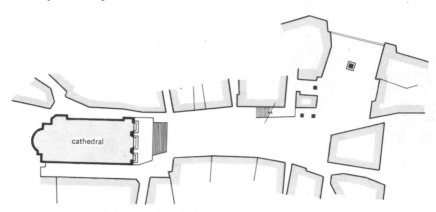

Town centre plan, Todi

to be called 'architecture'. But the fact is that many successful urban complexes have little if any building which can be dignified by this term.

Another interpretation of the theme is afforded by the interlocking squares of Piazzas Mantegna and Erbe in Mantua. The latter is the secular square bounded on one side by the Palazzo Regione and containing a massive medieval tower displaying a large clock made in 1473.

Main Square, Todi

Piazetta, Todi

Main Square, S. Gimignano

131

Cathedral Square, S. Gimignano

132

The space breaks open at one corner to reveal the smaller Piazza Mantegna, dominated by the gigantic west façade of Alberti's Church of S. Andrea. Separately the squares are undistinguished. The excellence lies in the dialogue between them.

This theme cannot be abandoned without reference to the incredible city of towers, S. Gimignano, to the north of Siena. The main square is almost a diminutive version of Siena, being asymmetrical and on a gradient. In it are the principal secular buildings. Once more another square opens off at one corner. The transition is effected by an open colonnade at this corner just sufficient to infer another space of contrasting character. The second square is small and austere by comparison, even though it contains the cathedral, approached by a wide flight of steps.

In the examples just cited, ambiguity is generated by spaces which can be defined as articulated. Another spatial formula with inherent ambiguity comprises serial squares. A sector of the medieval town of Annecy in French Savoie affords a good example. What would normally be a street is compartmented by lateral buildings, creating a sequence of miniature squares connected by low arches. Each square has a distinctive character, and part of that character derives from the presence of the arches revealing fragments of different spaces beyond.

Serial squares and arches, Annecy, Savoie

'Palladian' arch, Palazzo Uffizi, Florence

134

Epic Space

Arches can do more than just reveal space beyond, they give it a status. By affording formal limits to a panorama they elevate the framed view, giving it an 'epic' significance. That word is chosen because it implies heroic space, space which has been detached from its wider context and elevated well above the norm. John Nash exploited this device most successfully in his Regent's Park development, but one of the most impressive instances is the so-called Palladian arch which terminates the internal court of the Palazzo Uffizi, Florence. Seen through this most sophisticated of all Renaissance arches, the framed portion of the opposite bank of the River Arno is immeasurably enhanced in status. This is despite the fact that outside this frame, it is a quite ordinary urban panorama. As an effective frame to a formal, organized view, the archway to the Winter Palace in Leningrad has few rivals.

The Winter Palace and Alexander Column, Leningrad, seen through the arch of the General Staff Building (by permission of Theresa Prout)

Arch through old town hall, Bamberg, Federal German Republic

In the town of Bamberg additional flavour is provided by the dialogue between the baroque archway through the old town hall, and a vista of medieval roofs made the more interesting by routes converging from two directions. There is both a dialogue between foreground and distance and between the sophistication of the frame and the vernacular quality of the picture.

At S. Gimignano there is a variation on the theme of the arch. The route to the town centre passes through a high tunnel arch which is set at a tangent to the road. Consequently there is no vista, just deep shadow, reminiscent of Gordon Cullen's 'maw'. To the incentive to explore is added the bitter-sweet tinge of apprehension which darkness and the unknown evoke.

Arch to main square, S. Gimignano

Cathedral of Mainz, Federal German Republic

The use of arches and bridges both as means of communication and as visual devices which contain and liberate simultaneously, and give epic status to the space beyond, is guaranteed to heighten the impact of townscape. The complexities of function in the modern city would seem to offer much scope for this device.

When arches provide a frame to infinite distance, or sky, the impact is invariably profound, for reasons which are as much symbolic as picturesque. Epic quality may also be imparted by a foreground of straightforward buildings with 'heroic' architecture rising behind. This can be seen in Mainz where the Romanesque cathedral rises behind an ordinary square. The same dialogue in totally different styles can be seen in Lincoln where the vernacular architecture provides the foreground to the incomparable late gothic towers of the Cathedral, and in Limburg Cathedral. This is not without symbolic relevance.

Lincoln Cathedral

Limburg Cathedral

140

Teleological Space

Much of the appeal of historic towns is that they offer numerous goals for exploration. Previous examples were concerned with space which inferred the existence of other spaces. This section is concerned with *specific* architectural goals. A quotation from *Notre Dame of Paris* illustrates this aspect of urbanism:

In the medieval city no man saw the cathedral in its entirety – hence no man saw it like his neighbour. Because of the nature of the medieval city, each could see only portions, which were tantalizingly incomplete and which changed continually as the individual changed his position, compelling him to add the parts to form a total image in his mind.[1]

York Minster from Petergate – an example of a tangential approach to the central place in a medieval town.

Teleological space derives its impact from the partial disclosure of an object which implies a number of possibilities regarding its hidden shape. It is the aspect of townscape which gives scope to the imagination as well as offering incentive to exploration. Here, there is a connection with the appeal of ambiguity. The mind may delight in situations which offer a variety of interpretations. There is pleasure in constructing a total picture from a minimum of cues. Similarly, there is the pleasure first of anticipation and then of discovery when the imaginative construct is confronted with the reality. In art it is the technique of economy, of saying as much as possible in the most concise way.

Very little adjustment is needed to make the following passage by Arthur Koestler apply to an urban situation:

Economy is a technique designed *to entice* the audience into active co-operation, to make them re-create the artists' vision. To do so the audience must decipher the implied message; put into technical terms he must *intrapolate* (fill in the gaps between the 'stepping stones'); *extrapolate* (complete the hint); and transform or reinterpret the symbols, images and analogies; unwrap the veiled allegory.[2]

Because teleological space gives full reign to the imagination there is a creative transaction between subject and object. The perceiver injects life into the visible skeletal fragment; the partial disclosure acts as a thread around which he can crystallize his own images and symbols.

A recurring feature in many towns indicates a particular type of inference and incentive to movement and discovery. In many places the climax to the town is at the highest point both for symbolic and strategic reasons. In medieval towns, streets rarely give access to the central place axially; they approach it tangentially. The result is that the principal building of the square is only partially visible above the roofs. It is the magnetic fragment which offers the incentive to negotiate the hill to discover the whole story. This almost amounts to another urban formula. Rising above the curving approach-road to the centre of Villefranche de Rouergue is a most remarkable medieval tower of astonishing proportions. It turns out to be one of the fortress church towers found to be so necessary when the bastide towns were built in the twelfth and thirteenth centuries. From a distance, rising above the haphazard roofs of the town, its white stone stimulates all kinds of images. Here is the symbol of the Celestial City growing out of the chaos of the secular city. However sophisticated man has become, such imagery still has emotive potential. The Roman Ermine Street achieves the same relationship with the massive central tower of the Cathedral at Lincoln: a curving ascent to a partly revealed goal.

From within the miniature streets of Orvieto the tip of a pinnacle suddenly becomes visible. It is an indication that a special event awaits discovery and so image-building commences. But no imagination could

Approach to main square, Villefranche de Rouergue, France

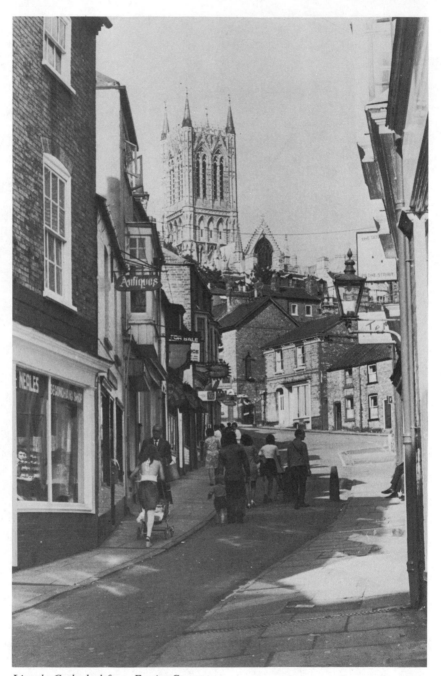

Lincoln Cathedral from Ermine Street

144

Street, Orvieto

145

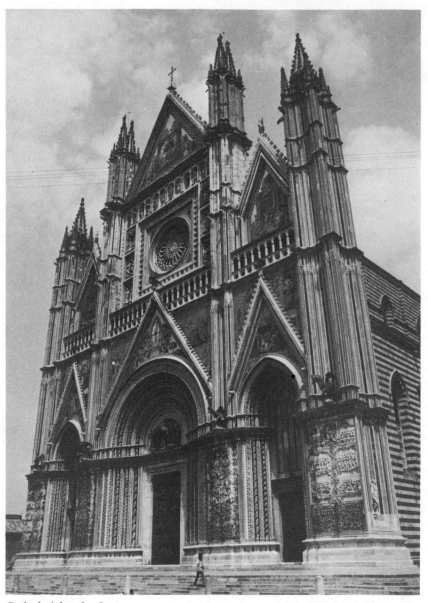

Cathedral façade, Orvieto

adequately prepare the way for the façade of the Cathedral, which is one of the most colourful and elaborate of any built in the middle ages.

Wherever you may be in Siena, the tip of the campanile of the Palazzo Pubblico is invariably visible, drawing you relentlessly to the town centre, just as the Cupola of the dome of the Duomo is inescapable in Florence.

Duomo, Florence, distant view

Duomo, Florence, from Ponte Vecchio

Inductive Space

There are places which, by their form and character, impel movement.
An up-to-date analogy is the linear inductive electric motor which
derives its energy *en route*. A street with a high incidence of *en route*
interest is an obvious example. Some of the downtown shopping streets
with wares displayed on the pavement are beginning to be appreciated
for their contribution to environmental interest. This is possibly because
they are so frequently replaced by modern shops which concentrate all
their assets internally. This is the fascination of the streets of Soho, concerning which, incidentally, there are rumours of redevelopment. No
doubt an application will soon be lodged to redevelop a prime site in
Westminster currently occupied by a very old and obsolete Abbey.

Plan of Assisi

Inducement to movement can be exerted by the form of the street. A simple curve can achieve this effect, especially if it is related to ascent or descent. When this configuration is associated with a special event seen fragmentally above the roofs, as in a street in Assisi, the effect is indeed dynamic. Being one of the most beautiful towns in Italy, Assisi merits more than passing attention. One particular route through the town

Arch in Via S. Francesco, Assisi

manifests so many of the qualities of dynamic urbanism. Ascending from the church of S. Francesco along the Via San Francesco, the first major event is an arch spanning the road adjacent to the elegant loggia of the Monte Frumentario. It is a prelude to a change of direction. The next accent occurs at the junction with a minor road entering from the left. This junction is greatly enlivened by pottery of all shapes, sizes and colours (see illustration on page 99).

Route along Via Portica, Assisi

Further along Via Portica, Assisi

Alleyway off Via Portica, Assisi

The road soon changes both direction and name, becoming the Via Portica. Having levelled off for a spell, the route now begins to climb sharply. Above the curving road, the tip of the splendid Ghibelline Tower of the People becomes visible above the cornices; exerting its teleological force. Along the road are shops displaying their wares externally, thus offering substantial *en route* interest. To the right, a narrow pathway drops away sharply, promising a most rewarding digression.

Finally the whole Piazza del Comune comes into view, dominated by the front of the Temple of Minerva, built in the time of Augustus. The square itself is a miniature urban masterpiece, possessing all manner of phenomenological interest. Routes open off the opposite end, with glimpses of the Cathedral of S. Rufino one way or the Church of S. Chiara (St Clare) along the other.

Ascent into Piazza del Comune, Assisi

Piazza del Comune, Assisi

154

Piazza del Comune from Via S. Gabriele

If one enters the Piazza the other way from the Via S. Gabriele the whole dynamic system operates in reverse, with the Ghibelline Tower acting as a polarizing object in conjunction with descent.

Accent to this characteristic of inductive space may be provided by some kind of architectural hinge. This is usually a cylindrical building or object which terminates a vista and simultaneously suggests that further interest lies around the corner. John Nash used this device in the approach to Regents Park, still to be seen in the Church of All Souls, Langham Place. With all the panache of later nineteenth-century architecture it is employed on the grand scale in the Museum, Walker Art Gallery and Reference Library sequence in William Brown Street, Liverpool.

William Brown Street, Liverpool

Complexity in Urbanism

An essential component of dynamic urbanism is complexity in its various forms. This may be regarded under five headings:

> geometric complexity
> shape
> texture
> relationship and rhythm
> decoration

Interest through geometrical relationship has been a design determinant at least since the Erechtheum was placed next to the Parthenon or Hadrian built his so-called Villa at Tivoli.

The interest behind a great many towns lies in the accidental geometrical relationships. Frequently, chance produces some of the finest interactions. An example is the perimeter fortifications of the town of Carcassonne. These emerged out of military necessity, but their aesthetic appeal was acknowledged in the last century when the defences were restored and improved by Viollet le Duc. Clearly there is no case for reproducing medieval fortifications, but they afford a compelling analogy for contemporary architects. Indeed some may be able to discern something of the shapes of Carcassonne in the forms of Manor Road United Reformed Church and Geneva Court, London N16.

Fortifications of Carcassonne, France

United Reformed Church, Manor Road, and Geneva Court flats, London

Architecture is now in a phase which favours geometric complexity. In less than two decades there has been a revolution in design and the scope of it may be seen on London's South Bank. Early fifties design is excellently represented by the Royal Festival Hall. Though a building of complex functions, these are all screened behind a simple outer shell. Adjacent to the Festival Hall is the Queen Elizabeth Concert Hall and

Hayward Gallery (see page 45), expressing the philosophy of the mid-sixties. Once again functions are diverse, but now these are reflected in the external form, and the interaction of different volumes produces the dynamic behind the design. It is 'ambiguous' design at its best and is complex and unpredictable. This philosophy made an agreeable entry into the seventies in the form of Sheffield's Crucible Theatre (see page 44).

The texture and colour of materials can often give emphasis to the form of buildings and so enhance their appeal. Part of the quality of Assisi lies in the overall pink and brown stone of rich texture. Vernacular buildings in old towns and villages illustrate the environmental quality which can be achieved inside a narrow range of shapes and materials. In

Saint Maximin, Gard, France

the Department of Gard, about thirty miles from the Mediterranean is the tiny village of S. Maximin. Here there is high eloquence in the simple relationship between shape and texture and the few terrestrial colours of walls and roofs.

Complexity of line as distinct from volume is a feature of places like Amsterdam (see page 101) with its rich gables drawn against the sky. Perhaps it is not just coincidence that Dutch buildings reach their climax at the point of contact between architecture and sky, since this country enjoys more of the latter, *pro rata*, than most other place in Europe. In the middle ages, architects delighted in covering their buildings with a profusion of lines. Externally this is seen in the Merchants' houses in the old square of Antwerp where façades are richly modelled by line and decoration. Internally there is no finer example of this design principle than King's College Chapel, Cambridge. Vertical shafts punctuate wall and window at high frequency, fragmenting into a myriad of ribs in the exquisite fan vaults.

Merchants' houses, Antwerp

Interior, King's College Chapel, Cambridge

Complexity of rhythm has already attracted attention. It can emerge spontaneously, as in Amsterdam, or by design. Rhythmic counterpoint has many modes of architectural expression and the examples of Antwerp and King's College Chapel exemplify the rhythm-principle geared to the complexity demand. In Amsterdam or Antwerp order is imposed by the lower frequency rhythm of the houses themselves, expressing their autonomy, with elaborate gables and staunchly independent storey heights.

Irregular rhythms in the context of a wider architectural order have become a popular current motif. Once again the panache of a master is probably responsible. At his monastic buildings at La Tourette, Le

Couvent de la Tourette, Eveux sur l'Arbresle, France

Corbusier integrates two rhythms most successfully. The fairly regular rhythm of the residential cells is expressed on the top two floors and imposes an overriding order on the building. Below this, a very high frequency, irregular rhythm is established on three floors by thin vertical slats; altogether a fascinating essay in counterpoint. Over a wide sphere of design Le Corbusier seems to have been almost obsessed by the tension between the ordered and the arbitrary. In the overall execution of so many of his buildings there is a complete paradox between the sophistication of the sculptured form and the almost rustic crudeness of its execution. Nature never entirely relinquishes its grip on his buildings, and the grass planted in profusion on roofs and decks suggests this organic relationship was deliberate.

Intricate complexity of form and rhythm contribute to architecture of a high calibre by Powell and Moya in the Cripps Building at St John's College, Cambridge. A linear building, it follows a serpentine course through lawns, woods and alongside waterways, contrasting forcibly with the formal architecture of New Court. Reference has earlier been made to the façades of Palladio's Venetian churches. There are not many pieces of architectural sophistication to match the superimposed rhythms of these integrated temple fronts.

The art of decorating buildings has been lost for the time being. Where efforts have been made the result is often unsatisfactory, since decoration usually has been applied to compensate for weaknesses in the basic design. We are in a period of pure shape, in which the appeal of architecture lies in the organization of its basic elements.

Cripps Building, St John's College, Cambridge

Traditional ensemble, Nantwich, Cheshire

164

However, at certain periods in history, such as the middle ages, the synthesis of form and decoration was successfully achieved. Especially in France the west façades of churches in later Gothic were a *tour de force* of architectural decoration. The marriage of structure and decoration was perhaps most perfectly achieved in the half-timbered houses of this period. They are seen at their best in southern Germany (see pages 106 and 107), in Cheshire, such places as Nantwich, and the extraordinary Moreton Old Hall. How a medieval street exhibits complexity on many levels is beautifully exemplified by Dinkelsbühl, Bavaria, with its variety of shape, colour, decoration and texture.

Dinkelsbühl Bavaria

This area of complexity must of course embrace the baroque. Aesthetically, complexity is sometimes equated with vulgarity. This is the inevitable verdict of the purists or classicists who have the 'high' view of art and design. But the aesthetic satisfaction to be gained from the saturation complexity of an interior like the Bishop's Palace at Würzburg (see page 93) is no less valid within its terms of reference.

Bare surfaces have always presented a challenge to fill every inch with some kind of activity – painting or sculpture – and Würzburg is the ultimate answer to this challenge as it introjects its extravagant ecstasy into the most sceptical of Protestant minds. The architecture of the baroque or the flamboyant late Gothic annihilates good taste with its confident vulgarity; it disengages the calm and rational mind from all its

Minor Square, Siena

anchorages and draws it into its seething vortex of activity. The great baroque churches and palaces are irresistable to all but the most inflexible or prejudiced, for they represent the ultimate expression of the limbic-centred complexity-demand. Whereas the other aspects of complexity have a strong element of intellectual appeal, saturation complexity makes its impact on the limbic brain, and so appreciation on this level may be tied up with other complex aspects of psychology and personality.

Ceremonial Space

The town or city is more than a utilitarian artefact. Historically, it was a visible celebration of the unity between man and the cosmos. This celebration was periodically reinforced by festivals and religious processions such as those that took place along the Panathenaic Way, culminating at the Parthenon on the Athens Acropolis. A town without any motivation to celebrate is merely an urban projection of a mood of pessimism.

Right up to the present century, towns were keen to celebrate their more illustrious citizens by statues and other artefacts. This was especially true of the Italians who seem particularly endowed with a capacity for civic pride. At the same time, statues serve to raise the status of a place. What might otherwise have been merely a leftover space off the main square of Vicenza becomes a piazzetta in its own right; a little bit of visual accentuation which helps to give shape to a town. Siena is no less eloquent in its minor squares.

Towns also may celebrate occasions. Vicenza boasts an architectural monument of totally uncharacteristic vulgarity for Palladio, the Loggia del Capitaniato built to celebrate the victory of Lepanto. Euphoria overcame good taste, and why not? All towns should have some occasions to celebrate – some event which enables the citizens to bask in reflected glory. London even celebrates the great fire with a monument erected by Christopher Wren. For him, more than any other, the fire was a cause for celebration.

National events or heroes also have a place in the hierarchy of civic celebratory artefacts. Few places in Italy are without some reference to Garibaldi. The last major outburst of statuary in Britain was in honour of Queen Victoria. Statues of her appear in many shapes and sizes and in diverse locations. Liverpool's Victoria monument also serves to mark the location of public toilets – a bi-polarity with which she would not have been amused.

Civic pride is usually most eloquently celebrated in the town hall or palazzo pubblico. The first to manifest this characteristic were the Italians, who, in the twelfth and thirteenth centuries built a spate of

Loggia del Capitaniato, Vicenza

town halls, expressing all the pride and self-importance of the city state. Florence and Siena possess superb examples, culminating in campanile which are really the ultimate in urban sculpture.

It is curious that it should be the Germans who have built the most spectacular modern equivalent to the campanile in the central tower of the County Administration offices, Bensberg, Federal German Republic. This is a fine piece of monumental urban sculpture which represents complete defeat for the cost accountants.

Landkreis Administration offices, Bensberg, near Cologne

Finally, most towns and cities still show evidence of the ultimate cause for celebration, namely the beneficent relationship existing between mankind and divinity. The religious centre was described in the context of symbolism. In Italian towns there is usually an equivalent and associated celebration of civic and divine allegiance. Elsewhere the cathedral dominates the town. Certainly in the middle ages a cathedral like

Cathedral of Chartres

170

Chartres was the focus of all urban celebrations, commercial, political and religious. Now the festivals have lost much of their significance, but the architecture remains.

Celebration through artefacts and festivals is part of the built-in therapy which can be provided by the polis, whether ancient or modern. The pay-off may not appear in balance sheets, but those who control spending on built environment should realize that the benefits will appear in other less tangible forms.

References

1 A. Temko, *Notre Dame of Paris*, Viking Press (New York, 1959), p. 159
2 A. Koestler, *The Act of Creation*, p. 341

15 The Passive Agenda

Because attention in recent years has focussed upon urban monotony, this has meant that prior consideration has been given to counteractive measures. As an answer to the security-demand, urbanism has been undervalued.

Yet the need for security and stability is just as legitimate as the validity of arousal, tension and stimulation. From the security aspect there are many ways in which the town can offer satisfaction. One of the original reasons for dwelling in towns was the protection it offered from powerful predators. Fortress hill towns exist in abundance as testimony to a troubled history. Now a city no longer has a defensive significance; indeed life inside Washington or Calcutta has its particular perils. Nevertheless, it is conceivable that the mind still subconsciously attaches importance to the protective aspect of urban life which is part of man's psychological inheritance.

What is undeniable is the fact that man feels security in a group. The town represents a concentration of people and so satisfies gregarious needs. In countries where this need is perhaps felt more acutely, towns offer many facilities for social intercourse. Perhaps it is not entirely coincidental that these places also enjoy a warm climate.

Historically, the town square has been the ultimate urban symbol of security. It offers total protection, and at times that protection can be excessive – the French bastide town of Villefranche de Rouergue is an example of this. In such places the visual force-system is centripetal. Contact with the wider world is minimal. Here the town square offers a magnified version of the security of the home.

The same message is communicated by narrow streets and 'cosy' precincts. The city of Leeds has recently turned a central network of streets into a traffic-free zone (apart from service vehicles at set times). The transformation is remarkable. However, the ultimate in pedestrian precincts is a pattern of streets, the Commercial Arcade, laid down in the eighteenth century in the Guernsey town of St Peter Port. Few places are more protective and congenial. Even the British become gregarious in a warmer climate, as evidenced by the High Street in the same town.

The city is man's absolute answer to the arbitrariness of nature. It symbolizes the triumph of order over chaos, and suggests to its in-

Commercial arcade, St Peter Port, Guernsey, Channel Islands

habitants that the vagaries of nature are permanently at bay. This suggestion is of course frequently undermined by natural and man-made catastrophes. Even so, cities such as London, Paris, or Rome appear to have a remarkable capacity for survival.

Rome has another attribute which contributes to this array of mental needs. It is a city which, perhaps more than any other, represents a continuum of being. Intermixed in a splendid way are artefacts spanning 2000 years. The fact that the past has been preserved so well offers a probability of preservation in the future, a characteristic which was more fully described under the heading of urban symbolism.

High Street, St Peter Port

174

Place Relatedness

Security is also associated with attachment to place. There is a tendency among strategic planners to play down the importance of place-relatedness as a contributor to psychological well-being. In the middle ages, the home town environment circumscribed the whole of life. The orbit of travel for most would be limited to the adjacent fields. The principal escape route was a pilgrimage, which must have had a variety of attractions apart from the religious.

Now comparatively few spend their lives in the town of their birth, and the place of residence is often regarded as a base from which to make expeditions of discovery. At his work the citizen may be involved in a super-local organization which does not specifically relate to his home town. The common currency of contemporary international architecture gives visual support to the super-local ethos.

Because the current life-style for so many involves time away from home and time allocated to commuting, social ties with a place are more tenuous than ever before. To recover from the stress of work and travel, it is often the easier option to relax in isolation in front of the television instead of reinforcing local social ties. Television itself is a super-local factor in the extreme. Many indeed are the factors which undermine the security of place-relatedness. The question is whether architecture can counteract this trend in individual and community terms.

Some would argue that the degree of social interaction between groups is more important than the physical quality of environment. They would quote the slum streets of back-to-back houses generating strong social cohesion and group allegiance. The argument might be pressed further by suggesting that the environmental deficiencies contributed to the strength of social cohesion through common hardship. Social harmony is never so strong as in a war.

Of course this argument makes Utopians turn pale, especially developer-Utopians for whom dreams of new environment are linked with large profit-margins.

Because the back-to-back environment is universally denigrated, its positive qualities are sometimes overlooked. Being a high-density, ground-level residential situation, it produces a high probability of face-to-face contact. Until the last war, families would tend to stay within a particular identifiable constellation of streets, which meant both strong family attachment to place and total age differentiation. In the streets off Scotland Road, or Granby Street, Liverpool, it was not uncommon to have whole street parties taking place on the carriageway. This would be inconceivable in Hampstead Garden suburb.

So, monotonous, grubby terraced houses became the backcloth against which elaborate social interaction took place. Their appearance belied the fact that every brick was saturated with symbolism for that social group. When the planners rolled them away like a worn-out carpet, generations of symbolism were suddenly disembodied. Because of the casualties created by the ostensibly enlightened process of urban renewal, we have now come to realize that an individual's or group's sense of belonging to a real place depends on two things:

Social experience and
Context

The context soon takes on the role of symbolizing the social experience. Considered in another way, the built environment, because of its capacity to become symbolically charged, literally *incarnates* experience. To destroy such environment is for many people a kind of psychological crucifixion, with no hope of a meaningful resurrection.

But towns and cities must renew themselves to stay alive. Urban renewal, since it is inevitable, must be conducted with the knowledge of peoples' needs. It calls for both imagination and compassion. Renewal is conducted against a background of a rapidly diminishing number of factors which may be said to define locality. This applies to architecture, institutions, and language. Just as local accents in speech are disappearing, so vernacular architecture has all but demised. Even if the vernacular content is eliminated, a particular organization of buildings and density and variety of their elements gives a place uniqueness. If it also forms the context for a socially-intensive event, for example, an open-air market, that collection of buildings takes on a powerful symbolic aura for the community.

At the time of writing, a battle is taking place to save Chesterfield Market. So successful is this market that it is recognized as a regional market for north Derbyshire. Its success is long-lived since it boasts a continuous existence on the spot since the thirteenth century. On the Continent this would not be cause for comment; in England it is a miracle.

It seems its days are numbered since the local authority has entered into an alliance with a developer – a formidable combination indeed. For centuries the sinews of social experience and human artefact have intertwined on this spot. By a simple Council resolution these sinews are likely to be severed, and so another Unique and Only Place becomes Anywhere 1974, with a massive mega-shopping complex, devouring ground and people. Practically the whole town signed a petition, to preserve the Market, to which the Council turned a Nelsonian eye.

Chesterfield is a parable for Britain, and indeed for Europe, with its vast heritage of historic towns. Such are the limitations of the modern architectural aesthetic, that in the hands of so many of its manipulators it reduces environment to a universal, lowest common-denominator.

Market place, Chesterfield, Derbyshire

There are exceptions. Eric Lyons, in apparent defiance of the Building Regulations (he must be made to divulge his secret) has created a lively and truly one-off centre for his village at New Ash Green. He is also building a new coastal resort town at Vilamoura, Portugal, in a manner which is full of character. This is another way of saying it is strong in elements which proclaim its uniqueness. Few architects in Britain have had more interference from local authority planners, for he is an individualist with strong views about the totality of the man-made environment. Vilamoura is allowing the freedom long denied him in Britain.

Recommendations

It is essential that the urban design agenda should show recognition of the fact that built environment has great social significance as the medium for individual and collective symbolism, and that attachment to place is an extremely important contributor to mental well-being. As social experience is unique, so the sense of attachment to place will be that much stronger if its architectural context is equally unique. This is the first recommendation, that with the explosion of super-local factors the international business corporations, chain stores, international architecture, and planning, etc., it is all the more essential that architecture and urban

177

New Ash Green, Kent (by permission, Sam Lambert)

Project for Vilamoura, Portugal (by permission, Eric Lyons Cunningham and Partners)

space should accentuate *this one and only place*. This means designing with heightened sensitivity to the 'genius loci' and thereby reinforcing the community.

Secondly, stemming from this, there could still be some social validity in the ancient symbolism of the labyrinth. Earlier the 'maze factor' was introduced in connection with its problem-solving attachments. The ancient significance of the labyrinth was that it put the seal on citizenship. Only the inhabitants of a particular place would know the key to the local labyrinth, and so it was a quick way of detecting hostile infiltrators.

A place that, overall, yields the secrets of its systems slowly confers upon the initiate a special status. As the internal mental model comes closer to external reality, so a relationship builds up between the individual and his town, and between the individuals who corporately share the secret. Knowing the inner secrets of a town reinforces the attachment to place, and the bond between those similarly attached. Contemporary planning and architecture are criticized because all their visual assets are immediately revealed. We should learn to build-in secrets, or allow scope for mazes to grow spontaneously.

Thirdly, locality emphasis is undermined by all the evidence and symbols of rapid movement. Towns, such as Birmingham (Great Britain), which have allowed full reign to the ambitions of their traffic engineers have abandoned all chance of building up a strong atmosphere of significant place. Not only are they inviting rapid entry to the centre, they are also encouraging rapid egress. Altogether they suggest that one's stay in the public and semi-public domains should be momentary, not only because the very presence of urban throughways denudes the place of interest, but also for the reason that they symbolize 'getting-away-from-it-all'. High capacity roads are lethal to any sense of locality or place.

It has been suggested that this frantic car-born mobility of this era denotes a desperate search for ultimate place where *real* social contacts can be made in a *real* context.[1] Perhaps this is so. Man still nurtures the myth of the perfect community, an earthly Zion, which is perfect in terms of society and urban design. Highway engineers reached a pinnacle of achievement in Paris. Now Paris is as much a place to pass through as arrive at. Its 'hereness' leaks out at high speed.

To summarize: urban form should reinforce social experience. Each town should be unique – assertive of its visual and spatial independence, and worthily symbolizing the super-image of the community. At the tactical level this is not just a matter of architectural form, but also of providing places for high-frequency and high-intensity social interaction.

Sense of place is reinforced by visual accents. Sculpture and intensified architecture in terms of variety and frequency of visual events should mark nodal points in movement routes. Towns should learn to celebrate their mere existence once again by indulging in things which give social satisfaction, against the grey-faced advice of the cost-accountants.

As time and space seem to expand in parallel with the expanding universe, and super-local factors give way to global factors and then ultimately to inter-planetary factors, a place to which an individual can relate, and which offers him a share in its image, seems more necessary than ever before. The town, even the city, is the last of the truly local factors in modern life.[1] Things even now are attacking its local integrity, and therefore everything must be done to optimize the things which proclaim *this one and only place*, this pivot of the universe.

Reference

1 See F. Lenz-Romeiss, *The City, New Town or Home Town*, Pall Mall (1973)

16 Limbic Values

In Part One, the general description of the cortical system included reference to the limbic brain. Since the brain is compounded essentially of systems and since they may well display different needs, it is important to consider how specifically limbic needs relate to the urban design agenda. Built environment should, to a degree, cradle the mind as well as stimulate it.

In the very broadest terms, the limbic system is biased towards security, though this bias can be overturned when more powerful emotions like love and hate become dominant. However, these are not strictly related to urban decisions.

To understand more about the design implications it is necessary to look a little more closely at the perceptual and evaluative capacity of the limbic brain, which was alluded to in Chapter 3.

In that Chapter it was stated that 'the mammalian brain can make complex discriminations without contributions from those structures upon which consciousness depend' (i.e. involvement via RAS of the neocortex) and furthermore, 'stimulus directed behaviour without consciousness is mediated by a phylogenetically earlier cerebral mechanism'.[1] Subliminal perception is not merely a diluted version of conscious perception. Experiments have shown that the primitive complex optic system can make contact with the verbal centres of the neocortex.

Both optic systems, therefore, make use of a common pool of stored information, but each demonstrates a quite different *attitude* to that information. The limbic system conceivably has its own criteria which evolved during the regime of the paleomammalian brain or mesocortex, before the neocortex was operationally significant.

It is possible to make further guesses at the criteria of the limbic system. First, there is evidence for believing that the limbic system has a strong preference for the exotic, and stimuli which demonstrate high figure-to-ground contrast. But there is also the implication of garishness as well as uniqueness. The limbic criteria attach value to things that glitter or display a rich variety of colour. This value system reached its ultimate form in the middle ages. The 'Celestial Hierarchy' was a treatise which proposed that objects had theological value according to their capacity to reflect light. Clergy therefore felt a divine duty to collect

Piazza of St Peter's, Bernini's colonnade

precious stones and metals, a duty they frequently discharged with efficiency and enthusiasm.

Another irrational but still effective criterion is the myth that size equals importance. This is certainly one of the factors behind the scale of certain human artefacts.

Two basic rhythms generate a lively response from the limbic brain. The first is an emphatic serial rhythm of comparative simplicity. It speaks through the drum beat rhythms of the tribal dances of primitive communities, and is a decisive ingredient of the pop scene in 'civilized' primitive communities.

Architecturally, the simple serial rhythm of the colonnades in Wren's Naval Hospital at Greenwich, London, and Bernini's piazza fronting St Peter's, Rome, activates this area of limbic sensitivity. Perhaps it is a matter of association with pulse rhythms which occur through nature at infinitely variable frequencies. The great railway viaducts of the nineteenth century still evoke deep-seated satisfaction because of their simple, heavy rhythm. Stockport is dominated by such a feature, and it means so much to the place that it is now the town symbol. In so much of this engineering architecture there is the element of gigantism which goes straight to the limbic brain.

The second kind of rhythm which generates a limbic response is high-amplitude binary rhythm, where there is a reciprocal and perhaps meaningful dialectic between opposites. It is impossible to detach this area of response from the complex and contentious sphere of symbolism. There are grounds for believing that spatial dialectics – height/depth, constriction/space, gloom/light, – activate circuitry, within the limbic brain associated with the collectively engrammed patterns of archetypal symbolism.

Professor Sybil Moholy-Nagy gives a clue to this limbic criterion when she describes certain design determinants of the Sumerians. They deliberately set out to achieve 'design contrast – the juxtaposition in scale, proportion, placement and materials, of singular monumental architecture and collective anonymous buildings . . .[2] Certainly towns and cities which display this visual bi-polarity have an appeal which survives all changes of architectural style and fashion. The appeal of high-amplitude bi-polarity seems to relate to limbic criteria and it is within the capacity of urban architecture to create this dialectic between opposites. Italian towns in particular exemplify this dramatic aspect of urbanism. They seem to concentrate into one great artefact so much of the vocabulary of urban dialectics, and it seems that it is the 'opposite-ness' as much as the symbolic meaning which satisfies limbic value systems.

It also seems that epic and ceremonial urban experience excites the limbic system as much as it does the cortex. Often scale is involved. As stated earlier man has always delighted in creating super-scale artefacts or environment which in turn confers upon him supernormal status. The Romans were accomplished at creating ego-enhancing architecture, and it was by no means absent from the motivation of the great Gothic builders.

Saturation complexity is a further phenomenon which appeals to the limbic system. It seems that the cultural cycle in the West moves from the Classic ascendancy of the cortex to the polymorphic (baroque) monopoly of the limbic system. Bavarian baroque churches exemplify this value system with their mesmeric confusion of redundant information. Old streets comprising a medley of form, colour, decoration, texture and people are the urban equivalent. Today it is the chaos of the market place, or the profusion of electrified advertising, which most commonly meets this demand. Regrettably, planners, ashamed of their limbic desires, seem intent upon eliminating this phenomenon from all towns and cities. Glitter, colour, complexity are all too vulgar to be incorporated in todays visually hygienic urban environment – 'pure as laundered sheets and just as dull'.

So the primitive, complex, optic system may activate the limbic system to attribute 'in an invisible manner' value and meaning to configurations of light and shade, height and depth, rhythm, space and constriction, size (the numinous), etc. Because the limbic system is also primarily responsible for generating emotions, experience of such configurations may be accompanied by vague but positive 'feeling' which may also have a visceral component.

The Temporal Sequence

The next step is to examine the temporal characteristics of the system. Colwyn Trevarthan brings out an important aspect of limbic perception:

If something unexpected moves outside the central field of attention, it registers first through the second, more primitive system before the classical visual system becomes aware of it.[3]

So the first stage of perception is subliminal and therefore obeys the primitive rules of the limbic system. The primitive complex optic system has a much higher neural transmission rate than the classical system and is not subject to a threshold of activation.[3]

Up to seconds later the classical system comes into operation through the RAS selecting data for conscious attention. Only a comparatively small part of the visual field receives such favoured consideration and, even then, perhaps on the basis of primitive rules.

As mentioned earlier, the RAS operates on the short term. With repeated stimulation, there is a progressive filtering out of stimuli deemed to qualify for conscious attention. This is habituation, 'a decline in innate responses due to repetition of the stimulus'.[4] In visual terms this follows the equating of data with the schemas of memory, or the modification of schemas to accommodate the new arrangement of visual events.

Once the habituation process has been completed, perception has reverted to the subliminal level. Reception, classification and evaluation of data are carried on within the limbic system, which apparently is not subject to habituation in the same way as the neocortex. Ursin, Webster and Ursin proved this experimentally in 1967. By means of electrical stimulation (of cats) they observed that the midbrain responded in full to an identical stimulus repeated 100 times.[5]

When, perception of the environment becomes the monopoly of the limbic system, it imposes upon incoming data its own particular attitude. Available to it are all the engrammed schemas of experience including urban and architectural schemas, but it views them in a primordial perspective. Its way of 'seeing' has not had time to be significantly modified by feedback from the neocortex. Five thousand years is nothing in the context of human evolution. So primitive matters of security and symbolism decide the style of the mental response.

This can be demonstrated by a graph comparing responses of limbic and neocortical areas.

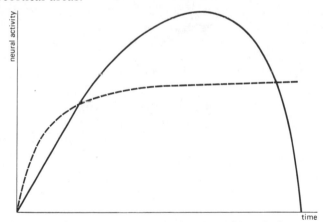

Rate of habituation – neocortical against limbic. Dotted line, limbic response mediated by primitive optic system; solid line, cortical response mediated by classical optic system

Design Implications

The involvement of the limbic system has two principal advantages. Firstly, it helps to offset the negative aspect of habituation. Secondly, it contributes to the fullness of the aesthetic response, which will be considered later on. In the face of the phenomenon of habituation, some have already suggested that it really is a waste of time expending effort on improving visual standards in the built environment. This view clearly rests on the assumption that habituation means a neural switch-off. The reason why the system of subliminal perception has been explained at some length (at the risk of labouring the point) is to establish that perception is a continuing phenomenon. The built environment, however familiar it might be, registers permanently within the brain.

It is clear from the graph that the limbic reaction may very well colour the conscious reaction of the neocortex because it anticipates it by up to several seconds. If there is sufficient stimulation to satisfy limbic perceptual needs, it generates a momentum which carries over into the conscious response.

The other point of great importance is that the limbic response continues after habituation on the conscious plane is virtually complete. If there is much information which communicates to the 'primitive' brain, this will gradually build up its significance as mental energy is released from conscious involvement. In other words, the depth symbolism of a place may only begin to register after the conscious 'intellectual' response has expired. So, if there is a rich matrix of limbic material in a particular built milieu, psychological attachment to the place may in fact *increase* in parallel with cortical habituation. The deeply satisfying groundbeat of archetypal symbolism becomes discernible once the complex melodies in the 'higher' register have faded away.

It is important for planners and architects to realize that people actually see with their gut, or what used to be called the 'visceral brain'. This may be the level upon which human beings really become attached to a place, and in an age when a premium is placed on speed, impermanence and super-local scale, it is essential to maximize the things which support place-relatedness. Maybe this way we shall effect a radical reversal in the usual evaluation of a city, making it a place to enjoy being in, rather than a low-profile hell from which to escape.

References

1 N. Dixon, 'Who believes in subliminal perception?', *New Scientist*, 3 February (1972), 252–5.
2 S. Moholy-Nagy, *The Matrix of Man*, Pall Mall (1968)
3 From an address to the 1969 International Congress of Psychology, London
4 The definition given by J. F. Mackworth, *Vigilance and Habituation*, Penguin Books (1969)
5 Described by Mackworth, *op. cit.* p. 75

17 The Symbolic Agenda

Conceivably the limbic system reaches its perceptual zenith when reacting to visual presentations which have overtones of archetypal symbolism. A truly twentieth century man like Deitrich Bonhoeffer might be quoted in his belief that man has now come of age and has no need of the ancient religious/symbolic support systems. In a strictly theological sense that might be true of a few advanced individuals, such as Bonhoeffer. In the more general sense it can be argued that ancient symbolic themes express themselves as vague, non-verbalized needs; they are part of the way of seeing of the limbic primitive optic cortex. Cities traditionally offered deep psychological nourishment within this emotionally-charged and deep-rooted area of need. Is this kind of nourishment still capable of satisfying a mental appetite?

To develop this theme first requires another look at the physiology and chronological development of the cortical system.

If neurophysiologists are correct in their assertion that actualization of the reasoning potential of the neocortex has only taken place within the last 5000 years, this means that the basic elements of archetypal symbolic themes were established in the collective memory during the regime of the mesocortex. The mode of storage of this system is of the 'picture-strip' or 'eidetic' type. Eidetic engramming has a high figure-to-ground probability, perhaps because the mesocortex is also the seat of emotions. Inevitably the early engramming of symbolic themes must have been associated with the release of emotions which were all the greater because they were shared.

If a symbolic language is passed on culturally for a few thousand years, and if it is eidetically engrammed, the chance of it becoming a permanent part of the mesocortical circuitry seems to be quite high. If genes can carry instructions about the circuitry of the deep structures of language, presumably through repetition, why not instructions regarding symbols?

There is an analogy in the development of children. Early memories are eidetically recorded because the neocortex has not achieved the stage of development necessary to do the job. As a result, childhood memories live on and can be recalled in great detail in old age. Indeed all through life, memories which have a strong emotional component, and therefore engage the mesocortex, have a high probability of achieving this permanent recall capacity.

A further important point is that the emergence of the first urban civilization coincides with the rapid exploitation of the neocortex. Thus Sumer appears to occur at the interface between the meso and neocortex. Its profound symbolism therefore may well be concretized at this interface which, in terms of future human development, is a most strategic position.

All this seems to amount to good reason for supporting Jung in his belief that the archetypes 'live on as systems of reaction and disposition . . .'

In such demythologized times it may be difficult for the rational executives of the environment business to accept that feedback from previous ages affects perception of the contemporary urban milieu. But the limbic brain not only exists but seems to contain circuitry which generates a psychological appetite for symbolic references going right back to archetypal origins. There are several reasons why it may be advantageous to acknowledge the relevance of ancient themes to the current planning and architectural agenda.

It has already been suggested that the contemporary life-style tends to undermine personal and collective attachment to place. High-speed mobility, high-speed change, high-frequency, low-impact information from communication media all operate against deep place-relatedness. It is no longer belonging *to* cities but escaping *from* them which is important to the urban inhabitant.

Some will question whether place-attachment is important. Others will argue that its absence may contribute to the mounting evidence of stress within the urban environment.

If the built milieu engages the mind on all levels, the chances of it stimulating place-attachment would seem to be greatly increased. By creating form and space which speaks the 'hidden' language of the limbic brain, the mind reacts in depth, and it is the experience of deep response which makes a place significant.

The limbic system is the seat of emotions and therefore when it is involved in a response, there is an emotional component which reinforces place-relatedness. Because of this there can be empathy between man and artefact which recovers the traditional meaning of the home-town.

This level of urban communication offers the possibility of contributing to social cohesion. Because the language of archetypal symbolism is primal and elemental, it has large areas which are common to particular cultures, races, even ultimately perhaps, the species. Therefore there is a high probability that an urban configuration which has overtones of archetypal symbolism will generate a collective response. Where a large section, if not all, of the community is perceiving environment on this level in the same way (in essence if not degree) this must contribute to the strengthening of social bonds through a communal and emotionally-charged attachment to place. The importance of this factor cannot be over-stated in an age manifesting the ascendancy of super-local media and organizations which are socially counteractive.

Historically, the shared language of symbols – the communally perceived meaning behind urban phenomena – was a decisive factor in cementing the unity of the polis. Even though the language is no longer consciously perceived, it may still be 'read' by the limbic brain through its own optic system, and so can help to achieve the goal of social- and place-community integration.

Chapter 7 described urban symbolism in the historical context and defined the broad categories of archetypal reference. It now remains to see whether they can be related to the contemporary agenda without prejudice to modern architectural design integrity.

A recent visit to the New Town (still largely on the drawing board) of Milton Keynes, Buckinghamshire, stimulated thoughts about the essential characteristics of cityness. This is a low profile development in the garden city tradition, without a hierarchically-distinctive centre.

Cathedral and city, Chartres

Approach to Duomo, Florence

·Earlier the organic analogy was used in support of the belief that towns and cities should be hierarchical artefacts. This also has validity in relation to archetypal symbolism. Perhaps they are not unconnected.

The symbolism of the 'centre' was universally exploited in historic towns and cities. Usually it involved creating a pyramidal profile to the city, with the temple or cathedral on the high acropolis. In both Chartres and Lincoln (see page 144), one is constantly being reminded of ultimate reality through architecture. A flat city like Florence still achieves this by means of its duomo, with its incredible dome dominating the city from all aspects. Its brilliant marble polychrome façade containing Giotto's elegant tower is a powerful reminder of the eschatological city of eternity emerging phoenix-like from the secular city. The administration complex surmounting the town of Bensberg has the same symbolic overtones (see page 169).

Hierarchical expression may mean the increasing scale of buildings, combined with ascent to an apex. The 'tone' of buildings also changes and they express enhanced status due to proximity to the centre. This may involve greater formality or an increase in the density of visual events by modelling or decoration, as shown by the approach to the cathedral, Burgos, Spain. In other words, the whole pulse of the place quickens as the centre is approached.

An attempt to achieve this symbolic effect failed decisively at the new town of Cumbernauld, Scotland. The whole commercial centre of the town was compressed into one building of singular appearance. In aspect it is formidable and uninviting, but the main reason for failure is the wilderness of space which surrounds it. The centre does not rise out of the urban fabric but stands like a citadel, separated from the community by a no-mans land which, in the prevailing weather, is closely akin to a moat. Clearly it was assumed that most clients would arrive by car, a luxury which few of the distaff inhabitants of Cumbernauld enjoy.

All this has implications for a high rise policy in towns and cities. In 1960 London was dominated by the dome of St Paul's Cathedral, which provided the pyramidal profile. Today this has been entirely undermined by the proliferation of towers spread evenly over the skyline. Had these been spatially concentrated, the hierarchical reference would have been maintained, albeit expressing the material priorities of the seventies.

The current predilection for the construction of towering buildings almost certainly stems from a degree of symbolic motivation. Primordially the tower was a means of escaping from the trials of earthbound reality and approaching the celestial realm. It is an expression of the archetypal appetite for gigantism. By associating with the scale of the super-normal one symbolically casts off the chains of mortality. Manhatten is an enlarged version of S. Gimignano.

Siena offers superb symbolic expression of the archetypal theme, liturgically expressed in rites of sacrifice, that ultimate life can only be attained via an experience analogous to death. The dialogue between constriction and space, darkness and light are just as capable of expression in modern urban architecture as in the style of Siena. Some British architects and planners demonstrate sensitivity on this wavelength, for example Eric Lyons in his village of New Ash Green (see page 178), Kent and Roy Gazzard, in his concept for the new town of Killingworth.

191

Approach to the Cathedral, Burgos, Spain

S. Gimignano, shown on page 137, exemplified what Cullen calls the 'maw'. This deep, dark archway has powerful archetypal overtones of the sacred cave, the primordial womb, etc. It is pure form and space; timeless architecture, for which there is no time like the present.

Finally, the penetration of water into the urban milieu has the potential to set up primordial resonance. In contemporary architecture it is frequently debased to mere decoration. At the foot of the twenty-storey

Thamesmead GLC development, South London (by permission of the GLC)

Arts Tower of Sheffield University is a rectangular pool containing about eight inches of water. A private gale generated by the building ensures that the pool is soon fouled-up with all manner of debris, and so it is now filled only on special occasions. Full marks should be given here for gross misuse of the elements.

A successful contemporary example of the incorporation of water into the built environment as a full partner is to be found at Port Grimaud on the French Riviera. This is a New Town built as a speculation, and designed in the maritime vernacular style of the region. In London, what is virtually the New Town of Thamesmead incorporates water in the total ensemble in a way which gives the place the authentic flavour of a resort.

So many towns and cities contain waterways in the form of rivers or canals. Because they have become relegated to sewers and conveyances for industrial effluent, their visual and symbolic potential is heavily veiled. Cities like Manchester and Sheffield could do much to enliven their central areas by optimization of existing waterways, a process begun by Birmingham. The confrontation between artefact and water has psychological significance far beyond the mere picturesque.

18 The Dialectics of Urbanism

As in Benjamin Britten's 'Variations on a Theme of Purcell', the instruments of urbanism have been depicted separately. In reality the real dynamics of urbanism derive from their combined orchestration. Curiosity and problem-solving needs stemming from the neocortex; the appetite for saturation complexity, serial and binary rhythms with archetypal symbolic overtones arising from the limbic brain – these all may find satisfaction within the broad dialectics of urbanism. Now it is appropriate to speculate how the relational principle can operate creatively or destructively.

The classical masterpiece of S. Maria della Consolazione at Todi may be a superb essay in design, but its real impact derives from the *relationship* between its cool classical symmetry and its environment; namely, a grove of trees on a hillside below the main town.

St Maria della Consolazione, Todi

S. Nectaire, Auvergne

The psychological reaction to this assembly of visual events is complex. The neocortex may respond to the classical purity of the architecture. The limbic brain gains satisfaction from the dialectic between human artefact and nature – the ordered and the casual. Here is established a high-amplitude binary rhythm, the kind of bi-polar rhythm which elicits a deep response, engaging intellect and emotions.

In the case of the little church of Saint Nectaire, near Clermont-Ferrand, there is great poignancy in the relationship between a human artefact of diminutive sophistication, and the wide arbitrariness of the

Villa Rotonda, Vicenza

King's College, Cambridge, from The Backs

196

Auvergne hills. The level-headed Greeks knew how to generate emotion by contrasting their supreme examples of architectural sculpture with a savage landscape, as at Delphi.

Andrea Palladio optimized this dialogue in his villas around Vicenza, the best known classic example being the Villa Rotonda. In eighteenth-century England, architecture was set within idealized landscape, carefully manipulated to create apparently spontaneous 'holons of elegance'. Of the numerous examples it is sufficient to cite Blenheim Palace, Chatsworth, Derbyshire, and The Backs at Cambridge. Men like 'Capability Brown' translated the paintings of Claude and Poussin into reality. When whole cities such as Salzburg (see page 68) are sited within a magnificent cradle of mountains, with their constant and often dramatic changes of atmosphere, the dialogue aspires to magic.

Present in such dialectic is the archetypal theme of order supervening the chaos of nature – of system transcending disorder. Here are foretastes of the ultimate mathematical perfection of the heavenly city, by whatever name it is called. When the dialogue is between water and artefact, the drama is increased. Here Venice must take pride of place. This city varies greatly in the tone of its relationship with water. At certain points it elevates the dialogue to heroic heights; at others the relationship is much less formal. The Dutch were supreme in establishing a low key, intimate, vernacular dialogue with water, in such towns as Alkmaar or Delft. Occasionally, in Amsterdam, there is evidence of architectural formality in relation to canals. The only major city in Britain, apart from London, which aspires to a ceremonial relationship with water is Liverpool.

Dialectics of *style* have never been so energetically pursued as in the present. We now seem to be firmly entrenched in the post-international-style era. Particularly in the United States and Britain, architectural assertiveness is transcendant, perhaps nowhere so positively as in university towns. The German Federal Republic has a fine contender with Bensberg County Hall (see page 169) in polarized contrast with small-scale medieval style houses. Where the international curtain-wall aesthetic was self-negating and anonymous, the current aesthetic favours heavily sculptured singularity. With the addition of the National Theatre, by Denys Lasdun, London's South Bank is now a showpiece for this kind of architecture.

Urban Drama

Just as the theatre appeals to reason and emotion, the same can be said of towns which exploit the potential behind visual drama. Siena has been quoted for its dialogue between low constricted arches, or high narrow approach-ways and the superbly generous Piazza del Campo (see pages 64 and 65).

Venice

198

Alkmaar, Holland

Raamgraght, Amsterdam

Pier Head buildings, Liverpool

National Theatre, South Bank, London

Havelot, St Peter Port, Guernsey

View of harbour from Havelot

202

This is urban drama at its best, containing like theatre, a strong symbolic component.

Assisi demonstrates how drama is experienced when urbanism unexpectedly breaks open to reveal a spectacular view into limitless distance. The Guernsey town of St Peter Port is built on a slope above the harbour. The result is that at one moment a street called Havelot is fully enclosed by high walls, and suddenly a break in the wall discloses a view of town harbour, sea and distant islands which is unforgettable. Even for the inhabitant it is a view which is never constant.

Underground Dialectics

It is possible for places to generate satisfaction through intrinsic relationships, even though on the conceptual level there seems little justification for this. This is because relationships are registering below the cognitive or stylistic level, on a plane which is perhaps just beneath the threshold of awareness.

The traditional townscape of the French Basque town of Bayonne exemplifies this principle. For planners who like proportions (window

Bayonne, SW France

levels, cornice heights, etc.) to correspond, it should be a nightmare. In fact, most people, planners included, would acclaim this as most pleasing townscape.

The reasons for this attitude are numerous. In the first place the town enjoys a high incidence of visual events. As contemporary built environment spaces-out its visual occurrances ever nearer the point of total monotony, places such as Bayonne, which satisfy the perceptual appetite, are increasingly in demand. What is so sad is that, with an adroit bit of 'doublethink', architects and planners see no lesson here for the present. Indeed, within this same visual array, the present makes its mark in a manner which is little short of catastrophic. Monopolizing about ninety metres of river front is the most undistinguished market and car park ever to hit a historic town.

This juxtaposition between old and new makes clearer what is the nature of the quality of the former. Though there is a high density of visual events, they occur at a fairly constant frequency. There is rhythm to this ensemble. It is a rhythm which sounds out its beat on the abstract level of *visual events*. Because it occurs behind the cognitive level of style and fashion, it is a matter of extreme subtlety. Nevertheless it is a powerful unifying factor. Things which are recognizable may bear little

Bayonne with fish market and car park

relationship to each other – unit size, colour, and shape etc. – yet an overriding unity can be established on the purely phenomenological level of visual events. This point entirely escaped the architect of the market. A 'visual event' relates to the 'noticeable difference', which is a definition within psychology and refers to anything which is able to be perceived in relationship to a context or neighbouring event. This has nothing to do with its conceptual association, and to analyse a particular urban array on this level may require converting the scene into a non-conceptual code which bears a direct but not point-to-point relationship with it. Something which might have potential here is the holograph produced by laser photography, which converts visual events into an abstract pattern. This may make it possible for an array to be perceived without cognitive 'noise'.

Density alone merely defines the quantity of visual events within a given array. Further complexity may be added to the rhythmic equation by a consistency in the *variety* of visual events. Not only is frequency involved here but also the rate of difference between events.

What this means can be demonstrated by a sequence of buildings in the Cheshire town of Nantwich (see page 164). Certainly there is rhythm in the density of visual events, but there is also constancy in their variety. Even more than Bayonne, on the superficial level this built sequence appears chaotic. Despite differences in style and the almost Disney-like distortion of walls, cornices and gables, there is a transcendant rhythm composed of frequency and variety, or rate of change, of visual events.

Once again, the qualitative aspect of this array is brought into sharp relief by the juxtaposition of a standard piece of developer's low-cost, high-return, nil-satisfaction architecture. Planning legislation in Britain gives power to local authorities to prevent this kind of thing, but the power is useless without the will, and it has been known for power to be tempered by the prospect of a good sale or high-rates income.

The final stratum of relationship on this abstract level is engendered by the *intensity* of visual events. If density can be equated with frequency, this is akin to amplitude. Concern here is with the *intensity of difference* between major elements of urbanscape. Such things as change of plane, depth of shadow, contrast in materials, colour, and texture account for amplitude or intensity. Rhythm here is generated by the inter-relationship of figure and ground.

How all these subtle underground relationships can be demolished at a stroke can be witnessed in King Street, Cambridge. The course of the street was laid down in the middle ages and much of its existing fabric is of this vintage. A consistent 'grain' is established by the harmony in terms of density, variety and intensity of visual events. This rhythm is shattered by the monumental rear elevation to a new block for Christ's College. Not only is it inimical in scale, texture (and all the other elements

Nantwich with developer's contribution

King Street, with new building, Christ's College, Cambridge

King's Parade, Cambridge

previously mentioned) to the ethos of the place, it also generates an independent line of direction, suggesting, with brash arrogance, that the days of King Street are numbered.

What is so disturbing is that certain architects and planners denigrate the fertile chaos of traditional street complexes such as King Street or, say, King's Parade. It is not inconceivable that some would prefer to replace the existing 'clutter' with the 'clean' lines of a modern comprehensive development of student accommodation. It is not a great step from King Street to the King's Parade hypothesis. These tacit dialectics, the underground rhythms and relationships, make a major contribution to the appeal of certain towns and cities. The matter of the overall dialectics of urbanism is clearly a multi-level concern embracing all the visual phenomena within the given frame of reference. It now remains to suggest conditions for a successful or creative dialectic.

As a first criterion, it is suggested that a creative dialectic occurs when the visual milieu conforms to the holistic principle, namely, that the total impact is much greater than the arithmetic sum of the parts would imply. So the first question to be asked about the contribution of a new or proposed insert into an established context is: does it enter into a creative dialogue with its neighbours in which there is mutual enhancement? The dialogue consists of elements both of agreement and contrast and is a

King's Parade hypothesis

matter of great subtlety and complexity. As words are blunt instruments, they can only hint at the nature of creative dialectics in the urban milieu.

In the most general terms, there are two types of dialogue which may be generated by new architecture. The first kind of relationship is that in which there is a sub-threshold transcendant serial rhythm uniting the whole array on the level of density, variety, and intensity of visual events. At the same time there may be the greatest possible contrast on the cognitive level, and so there is a creative tension between elements proclaiming unity and those affirming diversity.

Bensberg County Offices (see page 169) serve to illustrate the principle. Stylistically there is extreme contrast between the offices and the medieval style houses. The tower is a splendid concentration of visual events in contrast with the nearby restored medieval tower. Yet below this cognitive level there is affinity in terms of shapes and angles. There is a binding rhythm on the abstract level of variety and frequency of visual events. So there are numerous elements which contribute to high amplitude binary rhythms. At the same time there are sub-threshold serial rhythms which become more apparent when the total sum of relationships between the offices and town can be perceived.

The second broad principle of relationship is where the situation is dominated by a high-amplitude binary rhythm between a dominant element and subordinate elements. It is a tensile dialectic based on the contrast between figure and ground.

Before the Cripps Building was added to St John's College, Cambridge, the rear of New Court was a part of the College to be avoided, being in the best tradition of penitential architecture. Thomas Rickman piled all his architectural resources on to the elevation facing The Backs.

The situation has been transformed by the addition of the Cripps Building to the area behind New Court. Being visually complex (its elevations recall Mondrian) and irregular in plan, it contrasts in every way with New Court. The older building, being so restrained in style and economic in visual events, acts as a perfect foil to the Cripps Building, which sparkles by contrast. At the same time, the intense architecture of Powell and Moya encourages a reassessment of New Court, enabling its warehouse simplicity to be seen in a new light. So there is mutual enhancement (see page 163). Yet the dialectics do not end here.

There is a symbolic component in the perceptual equation. The brilliant white finish of the new building contrasts markedly with the grey of New Court, carrying the archetypal message of the ultimate 'city'. Furthermore, it is related in several places to water, achieving an almost Venetian dialogue where it reaches the River Cam.

St John's College, Cripps Building, elevation to the river Cam

All architects building in this situation have the advantage of an established and luxurious natural setting. The Cripps Building and Leckhampton House, off Grange Road, maximize this dialogue.

In a totally urban situation, Sheffield's Crucible Theatre (see page 44) exhibits this quality of being able to upgrade the wider area of its environs. It is a multi-faceted building, and its various elevations succeed in establishing a dynamic relationship with the diverse milieu on its several sides. On one aspect, the simple horizontal lines of the windows direct attention to the elaborate façade and tower of Victoria Hall, at the same time creating the suggestion of an irregular piazza. The same effect is achieved on the opposite side, with the corner of the Lyceum Theatre being the other principle partner in the dialogue. Here is a building with a variety of moods appropriate to the immediate neighbourhood, yet at the same time it is a coherent whole. Just as it has brought new life to Sheffield Theatre, so it has introduced urban drama to what was formerly an area of negative interest. People now want to preserve the Lyceum, thanks to the Crucible.

So far, attention has been focussed on dialectics in space. The same principle can apply within the time dimension. G. A. Miller was also earlier cited as believing: 'It is not enough merely to have energy falling on our eyes, ears, skin and other receptors; the critical thing is that the pattern of these energies *must keep changing in unforeseen ways*.'[1] (emphasis added).

It is possible to meet this condition by variability within the built milieu which may occur at different frequencies.

High-frequency Variability

Even long-term inhabitants can be surprised at the way in which a town can change its character from day to night. This is not merely due to the transformation effected when a building is internally illuminated, but other facets of the 'electric environment' such as advertising and floodlighting. Not only should high prestige buildings be eligible for floodlight treatment, but so should whole sectors of townscape. Patterns of lighting could be changed, creating a constantly varying *son et lumiere*. Urban sculpture is highly susceptible to change through variable lighting in both location and colour, especially if water is part of the ensemble. Sculpture itself can also be made variable, so that its form can be changed according to several permutations.

High frequency change is also effected by people taking over the urban space with festivals, fairs, markets, protests, etc. This is another reason why some urban space should be designated for monopoly by people.

We take things like changes in shop display for granted, but the cumulative affect of this can amount to considerable short-term variability, which helps to keep a town psychologically on the move.

Medium-frequency Variability

Wherever nature is incorporated in the built milieu, medium-frequency change is inevitable with the cycle of seasons. Also, planting may come into this category. Even trees can be moved about in a way which, a few years ago, was inconceivable.

Changes in groundscape are feasible at medium frequency. At present there is a vogue for creating pedestrian precincts, often accompanied by some primitive designs for floorscape. This medium-term change in the character of urban spaces is to be encouraged, as are contributions from shops which may regularly change their façades.

The motorist is the most unwilling consumer of medium-term variability, with sudden appearances of one-way systems which can add time and miles to a journey, sometimes without the benefits immediately being apparent.

Low-frequency Variability

Like the human body, towns, to stay alive, must renew their 'cells'. Low-frequency change is taking place in most towns continually as obsolete buildings are replaced. The principle of contingent optimization should ensure that there is a constantly changing and entertaining dialogue between the old and the new. This kind of dialectic has been achieved in places like the Universities of Oxford and Cambridge (the exceptions already being noted) and historic cities like Chester.

Low-frequency change concerns environmental modifications within an infrastructure which remains relatively constant. Towns which sacrifice their traditional infrastructure to the motor vehicle have usually been prodigal with their assets and will pay the penalty when feet are rediscovered.

Reference

1 G. A. Miller, *Psychology*, p. 34

19 Towards a Theory of Aesthetics

Perhaps the dialectic principle gives a clue as to the nature of the aesthetic response. During the course of describing value systems, it was proposed that all such systems depend upon the principle of significant relationship. Perhaps the point has been reached where it is possible to speculate about the nature of that significance.

It could be that the essence of the profound aesthetic reaction derives from the principle of binary mentation. Being semi-autonomous, the neocortex and limbic brain each manifest a coherent system of values.

Evidence that the limbic brain can be involved in an evaluative or aesthetic response is provided by the fact that there is frequently a visceral reaction accompanying perception. The impact of beauty may stimulate a moist eye or an indefinable sensation in the pit of the stomach. The limbic system exercises control over visceral functions as well as emotions.

Purely on the aesthetic plane, the neocortex, being the centre of rational processing, prefers visual relationships and proportions consistent with this bias. In broad cultural terms, as defined for instance by Jacques Barzun, this preference will be in line with the Classic tendency. This is the value system based on harmonic relationships in which the displacement between contrary elements is 'reasonable'. The 'classic' example is the ratio of $1 : \sqrt{2}$ which was canonic for architects in the Hellenic, High Gothic, High Renaissance and Georgian periods. In this artistic climate all opposites are reconciled and tensions resolved.

The neocortex searches for patterns of meaning in all phenomena, and so is nourished aesthetically by events which cohere into a whole much greater than the sum of its parts. In aesthetic terms, this holistic principle is also the principle of elegance.

The geometry of the Parthenon, St Nectaire, Auvergne (see page 195), or St Maria della Consolazione, Todi (see page 194), contributes to patterns of integrated events which are economic, pure and harmonic. All conflicts are resolved in an aesthetic value system which is supremely civilized. They follow the Vitruvium dictum that their form has absolute integrity which would be undermined by the least addition or subtraction.

The preferences of the limbic system, as discussed in Chapter 16, may be summarized as

1. the exotic;
2. saturation complexity with a high incidence of glitter and colour;
3. pronounced, regular serial rhythms and bi-polar binary rhythms;
4. gigantism; and
5. archetypal symbolism.

Emphasis on the autonomy of the two cortical systems should not obscure the fact that there is interaction between them. Maybe it is approaching an explanation of the aesthetic response to suggest that it derives from their simultaneous and harmonious involvement.

What is being proposed is that optimum value in mental terms is achieved when the mind responds to a visual array in *depth*. This means the engagement of the neocortex with its rational, classical criteria, and the limbic brain which enjoys more strident stuff.

The music of Bach is said to stimulate both intellect and emotion. The mathematical relationships of canon and fugue, etc., the overriding sense of serial order and coherent pattern, appeal to the neocortex. When this is directly related to a chorale of measured and profound simplicity and regular simple rhythm, the result makes a deep impact because here is a dialectic relationship between the complex and intellectual, and the simple and elemental. The human mind seems to get most out of dialectic relationships.

How this works in architecture can be demonstrated by the Piazza of St Peter's, Rome. Bernini's splendid colonnade forms the high amplitude contrast to the elaborate but highly organized façade of Carlo Maderna. The façade itself manifests tension between order and saturation complexity, the characteristic dialectic of high Baroque. Added to the equation is the regular high-frequency serial rhythm of the colonnade that ensures the participation of the limbic brain.

On a simpler level, the same dialectic principles are active when there is a market within an architectural setting. The formal, ordered pattern of architectural events as provided by the complex geometry of S. Lorenzo, Florence, generates creative tension with the chaos of human commerce and curiosity which provides the glitter, noise and saturation complexity beloved of the limbic brain. In Verona, the Piazza Erbe splendidly unites architecture and sculpture with the informality of the market place.

Earlier, reference was made to the music of Bach. In terms of architectural interiors, a close equivalent must surely be the Cathedral of Chartres (see page 77). At its rebuilding after the great fire of 1194 an ultimate masterpiece was demanded, and it must be the only case in

Piazza of St Peter's, Rome

history where such a demand was, if anything, exceeded. Succeeding generations have attested to the mystical beauty of this interior. Is this because it is rich in criteria of the limbic brain and neocortex?

Certainly there is a great deal to satisfy the new brain. In its order and symmetry it is quite classical. Vertical and horizontal are held in perfect balance. For a Gothic cathedral its economy of elements borders on the severe. Space is defined to give emphasis to pattern and coherence.

At the same time, by its scale, its breadth, as well as height, it evokes that response described as the 'numinous'. The limbic reaction is to massiveness, accentuated by the gloom imposed by deeply-coloured windows. Here is another facet of the primitive hierarchy of values, glitter and bright colour, set in an architectural framework of austere dignity. The whole interior is bound together with simple serial rhythms. Chartres achieves the ultimate in values impinging on the new and old brains, and therein must lie its magic.

In a different era, the same can be said of the pilgrimage church of Vierzehnheiligen, Franconia, by Neumann. In its decoration it yields to the Baroque value system which is limbic-orientated in the extreme. But transcending this surface froth is an architectural spatial order of a high

Market at S. Lorenzo, Florence

215

Piazza Erbe, Verona

Vierzehnheiligen Church, Franconia

Piazza of S. Marco, Venice, with Campanile

degree. There is a most successful dialogue between saturation complexity and intellectual sophistication which has earned for this church the term 'architects' architecture'.

The principle of dialectic relationship reaches ultimate expression in the wider context of urbanism. The Piazza of S. Marco (see also illustrations on pages 127–9) has been described for its quality of spatial inference. This only accounts for part of its appeal. On the neocortical side it is an ordered space, coherent and elegant. At the same time it stimulates curiosity drives.

Despite its intellectual sophistication, there are many things about the Piazza which have potential to satisfy limbic criteria. On three sides the space is defined by buildings articulated by high-frequency serial rhythms.

They propel the mind towards the façade of the cathedral which contrasts with them on every level. So there is also a binary, high-amplitude rhythm established between the cathedral and the other three sides of the square.

The façade of the cathedral itself is a fine example of saturation complexity, given greater limbic emphasis by liberal amounts of gold leaf. Further bright colour is added by the three enormous flags; heralds of the glories of the cathedral, and symbols of the majesty of Venice.

The limbic appetite for gigantism is amply satisfied by the great campanile which has all the qualities of the numinous. At the same time another binary rhythm is set up between the predominantly horizontal and highly complex cathedral, and the austere verticality of the campanile. Spaces discreetly open off the square, offering the prospect of saturation complexity of shapes and merchandise, and narrow spaces, vibrant with limbic symbolism. An important factor which impinges on the limbic level is the concentration of humanity displaying its own particular kind of saturation complexity and at the same time satisfying participatory needs. Even the pigeons contribute to complexity and movement.

Finally, this whole urban system embraces the sea with heroic confidence, a confrontation imbued with archetypal associations. Because so much of its communication is with the limbic brain, this space seems to be largely resilient against habituation, since the limbic system appears to maintain a full response, despite repeated stimulation.

Altogether this Piazza is capable of generating a profound psychological response. Here there is rich interaction between neocortical and limbic visual criteria inducing a many-sided aesthetic response. It plays cerebral games like disclosing fragments of potentially rewarding goals and resonates along a profoundly significant symbolic wavelength. Its very age symbolizes a continuum of life and activity following a consistent pattern over many centuries. And it vibrates against the water. No wonder Venice is universally irresistible.

Conclusion

It appears that the principle of *relationship* pervades all value systems. This is true of the value systems stemming from each cortical system. It is more profoundly true (that is relationships are more psychologically significant) when the principle of relationships unites the responses of the neocortex and limbic brain. Ultimate aesthetic value seems to depend on the dialectic between bi-polar events.

This can be demonstrated on the level of individual architecture where there is tension between the unity of the whole and the autonomy of component parts. This is a game which architects are enjoying at the present time, the dialogue between 'form follows function' and form equals unity or coherence.

Across the broader urban spectrum the often subtle dialectic between rhythm and pattern serves to satisfy the mind in depth. 'Dynamic' or 'kinetic' space sometimes generates a high amplitude binary rhythm which motivates movement, perhaps due to the visible fragment of a goal which infers substantial rewards.

This has amounted to a speculation that the brain operates a hierarchy of value systems in relation to visual responses. Value seems to increase the more the neocortex and limbic brain are simultaneously engaged in the response. Furthermore, evaluative criteria seem to favour situations which engender a kind of reciprocal or cybernetic relationship between the two brains which overcomes the dichotomy intrinsic to the system. Phylogenetic development seems to have created a situation in which conflict between them has a higher probability than harmony. The ultimate aesthetic response owes its profundity perhaps to the fact that it provides an answer to the 'dialectic of neurosis' or 'schizophysiology'. When an array of visual events generates complementary rhythms which integrate the two mental systems, then perhaps aesthetics becomes therapy.

A final point: it is conceivable that the cultural cycle, as described in Chapters 8 and 10, is the outcome of a constant shift from relational values which reside largely in the neocortex, the classical value system, to values predominantly limbic in nature: the polymorphism of saturation baroque. Cultures seem to oscillate between periods of neocortical and limbic ascendancy. To be more precise, the neocortex periodically reacts against the discreet regime of the limbic system, with an onslaught of rational ideals and classical visual values. Once the ideal is achieved, limbic criteria gradually take over, assisted by the habituation factor within the neocortex which can only briefly endure perfection.

For a designer it is important to recognize and conceptualize this tension. He, himself, is within a cultural system which, in terms of value criteria, is constantly on the move, and it could be highly advantageous to recognize why there is movement and to where it is leading.

In a sense, beauty in architecture – in anything – might conceivably promote optimization of the mind through the fact that in *creative* tension the human brain has enormous perceptual and creative potential. There is beauty in ethereal, disembodied classicism. There is beauty also in saturation complexity. But ultimate beauty occurs when they come together; when classicism comes down to earth and when 'polymorphism' is placed within the context of a transcending order.

These have been just a few of the ways in which towns can stimulate interest and sustain awareness. A town is a large enough artefact to embrace a host of opposites. It should be a place of security and peace as well as exciting teleological, exploratory and problem-solving drives. It is large enough to embrace diverse value systems. Altogether it is a visible expression of humanity in microcosm. Mental satisfaction is maintained, despite habituation, if a place is multi-dimensional in its mode of communication. The satisfaction becomes even more profound if the place is also tuned in to the primordial symbolic wavelength.

Part Three
Mental Strategies in Urban Design

20 Current Design Methods

As the perceptual strata of townscape has been considered in miniature, and an approach to design which is grounded in psychological needs and aspirations has been advocated, a design strategy which is most likely to elicit solutions which will meet these needs shall now be proposed.

The secrets of design in the architectural and urban context cannot be imparted in a few pages, even supposing they were possessed by the writer. It is, however, possible to suggest a broad strategy which can accommodate the variety, complexity, and paradoxes which are essential ingredients of an organism as massive as a town or city. At present, design philosophy on this scale tends to produce dinosaurs, massive but over-simplified organisms incapable of adapting to changing situations, and rather ugly.

Really it is a mental attitude to design which is being propounded, and therefore should not be compared with detailed methodologies which are available to architects. Design in the urban environment calls for mental strategies which maximize the various capacities of the mind at the appropriate time.

In general terms most architects use one of three design strategies, though elements of the other two are bound to be present. They may be defined as the

Inertia method
Scientific method
Intuitive method

Inertia Method

As the name implies, the inertia method is a most convenient strategy calling for minimum decision-making. It is a system of solving new problems with old answers, and is currently more prevalent than is readily admitted. In a period of overload it is tempting for architects to save time and production costs by using previous designs *in toto*. They are encouraged by over-paternalistic governments who tempt them with specimen designs for housing and compel them to conform to certain dimensions and grids.

In a building type which is heavy in mechanical services, such as a hospital or laboratory, it may make sense to repeat design decisions, provided there is room for feedback and development. There is no excuse for the local authority which repeats its dull housing types *ad nauseam*, corrupting the environment with crippling monotony.

Inertia processing in architectural offices is becoming increasingly popular. Up to a point it is rational to use standard details. Some architects design with a kit of parts, using different permutations each time. This is a subtle form of inertia processing. With respect to the system-maximizing principle of the brain, there is inherent danger in standardizing production details, since the more they are used, the more difficult it becomes to abandon them.

Scientific Method

The scientific method, as traditionally understood, is a design strategy which became highly developed in the sixties. Several people, notably Christopher Alexander, carried it to logical extremes, and it still exercises a fascination for those who adopt a rationalist view of science.

Scientific method is a means of tackling a problem by the strict laws of logic, and proceeding in a straight line towards a predictable solution. It therefore could also be called a serial design method. This method operates according to a system of rules and utilizes that invaluable mental facility, the consistency-demand. The design problem is atomized into its components, each of which is regarded as a separate problem to be solved. After each element is developed it is added to the design equation and the new whole tested for illogicalities. Design within this mode is primarily a matter of synthesis; rationally designed components such as plan, structure, services, elevations, are successively integrated into the scheme.

Scientific design method is committed to a mental procedure sometimes known as 'momentum processing'. Unlike inertia processing it disdains to resort to facsimile reproduction, but in common with it there is a strong commitment to the past. The existing arrangement of information is used to provide the *system* by which the new design is synthesized. Consequently, under the rules of the mental system, scientific design method is incapable of achieving a radical breakthrough in design. Logic and innovation do not readily co-exist.

The method appeals to designers strong in technology and weak in imagination. It offers an impressive framework within which information can be processed to the extent that it can induce a false sense of creativity. Once the method is carried out in every detail there is a temptation to expect a design to emerge automatically. Frequently, students, when first introduced to scientific method, founder on that particular rock.

Personality comes into the matter. This method is naturally attractive to the logical thinker who proceeds by induction. Such a personality is sometimes impervious to external criticism and quite incapable of self-criticism, characteristics which occasionally result in monumental illogicalities. Furthermore, there is a danger that this method will encourage the architect to proceed, by avoiding small mistakes, to the grand fallacy (to adapt a McCluhanism). Men who use this restricted definition of scientific method are temperamentally unsuited to being fallible, with the result that urban environment now has more than its fair share of grand fallacies.

Urban design is increasingly becoming the province of rational sciences. Because in the past architects have tended to be regarded as unscientific, economists, geographers, surveyors, etc., are now entering the lists in large numbers to redress the balance. The 'life-force' of the town and city is being clevery analysed so that its essence may be extracted, encapsulated and then distributed to all urban designers. The sphere of planning is being monopolized by scientific people who honestly believe that good design can emerge from atomistic analysis of the many factors which comprise urban environment. They find it hard to acknowledge that a scientific method of synthesis is alien to real creativity; its atmosphere cannot support the flame of imagination. Such a design procedure can organize material excellently; it cannot make discoveries. Architecture should never be confused with efficient building.

There is not space to speculate why this is so, except to suggest that conscious rational thought is compelled to move in a straight line towards a specific goal, because of what psychologists call 'focal awareness' and commitment to high probability patterns. At any one moment attention covers a minute area of the memory-thinking area of the brain, analogous to the fraction of the visual field which is in sharp focus on the retina. Creativity consists of bringing together areas of memory which have hitherto been separated under the prevailing organization of information in the brain. Focal attention cannot therefore embrace disparate schemas of memory. Furthermore, because scientific method is committed to the existing arrangement of information in the mind, it inevitably succumbs to the system-maximizing principle. This can be witnessed in scientists who refuse to abandon their intellectual position long after the concensus view regards it as untenable.

Times have never been harder for the architect. He must provide progressively improving environmental standards. At the same time he has to contend with litigation-minded clients, voracious contractors, and mean ministries. In the face of all this, and the explosion of technical information, he is easily tempted to become 'scientific' in his approach to design.* Technology is presented as the saviour of environment, a vision tainted a little by the suspicion that certain technological experts seem to work to tolerances of roughly plus or minus 100 per cent. However, that can be dismissed as prejudice born of nostalgia for less complicated times. In this maelstrom of essential data, a scientific approach to design is offered as the only chance we have of producing rational environment out of it all. But perhaps rational environment is what is causing all the trouble; the most successful towns in visual terms are anything but rational.

Intuitive Method

There are still some who accept the validity of intuitive design methods. Superficially, it is the antithesis of scientific method, and so is condemned by those who are committed to rational processing. Alledgedly this method is confined to certain neolithic members of the profession who refuse to step into the post-machine age. What is more, they are occasionally successful and even rather rich. That alone is sufficient to discredit the method.

The image of the intuitive designer is of one who enjoys communion with his Muse, periodically receiving flashes of insight, and eureka, Ronchamp! Undoubtedly some architects believe themselves to be favoured in this way. But this charismatic design method is unconvincing in such demythologized times, and in any case, it is impossible to teach.

The intuitive designer is one who allows unconscious information-processing to dictate a conscious solution. Alvar Aalto is said to conceive a design at very high velocity. It coheres rapidly in his mind as he traverses the site having first digested the brief. What happens in his case is that a lifetime of experiences together with information relevant to the precise job, all interact in a creative way, with a minimum of conscious executive control, to produce an answer. Because of this talent his answers are usually good.

Intuitive design methodology is sometimes vulnerable to the charge that it results in buildings which are deficient in those areas which call for logical processing. Against this charge many of the more exotic and idiosyncratic of contemporary buildings have no defence. The intuitive designer, because of his very facility, is tempted to reach premature three-dimensional conclusions. On his side he is a little contemptuous of technology, believing that it is the job of the technologist to adapt to the demands of the architectural maestro. So, intuitive designers have been known to be light on input, but this does not negate the importance of unconscious processing.

* There is no intention here to denigrate true scientific method which merges with art, as will be shown below.

Unquestionably the non-conscious strata of the mind are where man's real creative potential resides. The list of great discoveries and innovations which have been conceived quite unexpectedly, or through dreams or reverie, is endless. When the mind is allowed to freewheel it covers an astonishing amount of ground.

The intuitive designer exploits this problem-solving capacity of the unconscious mind. The mode is not without its hazards since there is temptation to regard the product of intuitive processing as having some mystical infallibility. Solutions to design problems which emerge out of the mists of inspiration are prone to be invested with a semi-religious authority, and so to criticize them is to commit heresy; understandably, since they come from some transcendental pool of information!

Intuitive designers have a built-in tendency to operate against the best urban design, for the reason that they usually think in one-off terms regarding buildings. They have an atomist view of environment. Their inspirational philosophy tends to make them aim at architectural masterpieces with each commission. This can undermine the total coherence of the wider urban context. An example is Cambridge (G.B.). Because of the prestige of the place, architects commissioned to design within its hallowed boundaries feel compelled to rise to the occasion and extract from themselves every ounce of design capacity. The result is a collection of buildings which range from the excellent to the outrageous. In the majority of cases, architects have been intensely individualistic, heavily projecting their particular design image. The result is fragmentation. Two recent colleges which we may presume to have a similar function stand side by side in Huntingdon Road, yet they could originate from different planets.

Cambridge is renowned for the Backs, the superlative piece of landscaping and architecture along the River Cam. The climax is King's College with its Chapel and lawn. Next to it, in a lower key, is Queens' College, built in the warm, domestic style of the fifteenth century. Beyond this is Silver Street bridge, from which the river used to meander into countryside, merely flanked by two pubs, The Mill and The Anchor. It was a perfect architectural diminuendo. Now, beyond The Mill, there is a 'progressive' piece of city-centre architecture accommodating non-collegiate staff. A superb architectural sequence has been destroyed. In terms of Haydn symphonies, it is as though the surprise bit of the 'Surprise Symphony' has been grafted onto the end of the 'Farewell'.

Another case is Brasilia, the most splendid of all modern non-cities. There is no sense of urban cohesion in this collection of magnificent pieces of architectural sculpture. Real town life occurs in the unplanned shanty town which inevitably emerged close by. Brasilia is meant to be looked at, preferably through slides; it is not a place actually to inhabit.

Queens' College and staff club, Cambridge

This is not to say that scientific and intuitive processing do not have a role to play in the urban design process. Each has deficiencies. Scientific method is incapable of generating a really imaginative response to a design opportunity. Intuitive method frequently lacks the element of discipline and control which is needed if buildings grafted onto an existing environment are to be organically assimilated. Too often, in transplant terms, rejection takes place. Therefore, it remains to propose a policy which makes use of their positive attributes whilst being alert to those facets which are 'counter-productive'. A method is needed which releases design potential in the architect and planner, to enable those with talent to do even better, and to encourage those without talent to be brave enough to recognize the fact and become administrators.

21 Towards a Strategy

It is possible to believe that shortcomings in the architectural and urban design process stem from yet another facet of neurophysiology. Until now the binary character of mentation has been confined to the dialectic between the neocortex and limbic system. But the neocortex itself is constructed on a binary basis, comprising left and right cerebral hemispheres.

The hemispheres are proficient at different tasks. The left cerebral hemisphere has an aptitude for verbalization and rational decision-making. Its neighbour is more efficient at dealing with non-verbal, spatial, abstract information.

Some recent research has shown a further divergence between their preferred modes of operation. It appears that the left hemisphere is proficient at serial processing, whilst the right hemisphere is better equipped to view things as a whole.[1]

For some time it has seemed that the technology-intensive culture of the West has been biased in favour of rational serialist or atomist processing. This is particularly manifest in the sphere of education. Thus there tends to be imbalance in the use of the cerebral hemispheres.

What really does give cause for alarm is that there is evidence to suggest that this imbalance could be genetically determined. It has been observed that by the sixth month of pregnancy the infant brain is, in many cases, asymmetrical, the left hemisphere being significantly larger than the right.[2] This has been confirmed by Luria. This could be a sinister situation because it means that the dice is loaded at birth. By the rules of positive feedback, strong systems get stronger.

This has been mentioned at the outset because design processing requires full participation by both cerebral hemispheres. Indeed it could be argued that the spatial, non-verbal, holistic bias of the right hemisphere has even more value in architectural design than the verbal, rational skills of the left hemisphere. Here is a challenge for the educationalists in architecture and planning to overcome a biologically biased situation. At present, architectural and planning education certainly tends to be atomistic or serialist both in its structure and philosophy.

As the subject becomes increasingly complex there is teaching input from a variety of specialists. Their contributions comprise a growing number of adjuncts to the core process of manufacturing architects and planners. By this system it is hoped that students will have deeper insight into a wide variety of ancillary facets of the design agenda.

In this it is probably successful, but possibly at the expense of side effects which may negate the advantages gained. For example, input by specialists with their own particular expertise may assume importance in proportion to the effectiveness of the exponent. At the undergraduate stage, students have not developed the facility to distinguish between ultimate value and propaganda.

An even more dubious result is that this process tends to establish an atomist ambience which tacitly conditions thought and executive activities.

Perhaps it is inherent in the nature of the academic to think atomistically, that is, in indivisible parcels of knowledge, and this attitude to information is inevitably communicated to the student. Certainly in universities there is a bias towards the atomist, analytical mind. Within the complexities and paradoxes of the architectural personality, this emphasis leads to a distortion which undermines creative design.

Perhaps the atomist attitude is most clearly demonstrated in the wider context of urban design. The need to acknowledge neighbouring buildings is generally conceded. Unfortunately, those conditioned to think atomistically try to achieve integration in a self-conscious and contrived manner. So there are superficial attempts to reflect the wider environment. In Spence's Erasmus Building for Queens' College, dark-red brick and the neo-Tudor arches are devices employed to integrate the building into one of the finest architectural contexts in the world. It is at the more distant focus that questions arise about its compatibility with its context, especially at roof level (see page 91).

Finally, the atomist climate of thought penetrates to the highest strata of planning, the new towns. So far, every new town in Britain eloquently testifies to logical, compartmentalized decision-making. Problems have been solved in a serial fashion according to a strict canon of rules – the prevailing hierarchy of planning criteria. As a result, it takes quite an effort on the part of human beings to invest some of these places with life. Sometimes a conspiracy between architecture and climate defeats human adaptibility.

What an irony it is that so many places conceived as Utopian ideals end up as routine pieces of doctrinaire overplan. But then the logical, atomist designer cannot leave anything to chance.

There is, of course, no instant medication which can cure these ills, but a measure of prophylaxis can be provided by a fundamental alteration in approach to all problems relating to the built environment. As before we must begin at the source, architectural education.

A beginning should be made by changing the logistics of the architectural and planning courses. Particularly is this relevant to specialist input which should be so arranged as to contribute to the holist concept of design. The design procedure in architecture and urban design should not be regarded as a matter of linear development but of *bringing a solution into progressively sharper focus*. This sharpening-up process must involve increasingly specific input, which comes from all directions. However, the global integrity of a project will not be undermined if this input is injected into the problem in the context of a holistically conceived agenda. The end result is invariably conditioned by the frame of mind providing the matrix of conception.

A good analogy is offered by the natural process of conception, birth and maturation. The development from feotus to adult is a matter of progressive definition. The feotus is a kind of thumbnail sketch with a 6B pencil, but all the essentials of the finished product are there. As it grows, the characteristics of the organism are more and more clearly defined. It is a progression from 6B to 4H. (These graphic polarities were not derived by measurement!)

This is not to underrate the value of specialist input to the design agenda. No criticism is implied of specialists who must possess selective vision. There is no such thing as a wholist specialist. It is the responsibility of the architect or urban designer to effect any necessary change of key from selective speciality to wholist application to the total agenda. This is not so much a skill as an *attitude* which must be shaped from the earliest days of professional education.

All the levels of manifestation previously discussed will be conditioned by this fundamental attitude. Individual buildings designed wholistically have a better chance of resolving the tensions between the diverse interests – plan, function, services, structure, and shape – the parts have a higher probability of cohering to produce a solution the significance of which greatly exceeds their arithmetic sum. So many contemporary buildings appear to have been *assembled* in design terms, and can never be more than a federation of parts. A physical organism offers an appropriate parallel.

An organism consists of a vast number of components, each comprising a semi-autonomous universe, yet intimately related to a higher whole within the organism. The balance between individuality and participation is critical. The same rule applies to the components of architecture.

The next stage in the environmental hierarchy is the urban subunit. The wholist approach has particular relevance to the problem of inserting new architecture into an established context. Ever since Hitler effected major modifications to our townscape, the complexities of relating new work to an existing milieu have taxed theoreticians and practitioners alike. Some architects, as has been mentioned, are spendidly free from such constraints, but the majority feel obliged to nod deferentially to the immediate context to their buildings. This has been called 'inflexion' or 'good manners', and rarely has this approach concealed the self-consciousness from which it has been conceived. No one is really taken-in by corresponding storey heights, identity of materials or stylistic similes.

The wholist designer should be able to absorb the ethos of a place and allow it to become an essential part of the design agenda; so much so that it exerts a decisive influence upon the final concept. This way there is a chance that the new insertion will be a creative addition to the total milieu by expressing the autonomy/participatory tension in terms that are subtle and discreet.

The final area of relevance concerns planning from the neighbourhood to the whole town or city. Here the basic dichotomy has been between strategists and tacticians. These are the two giant atoms comprising the design agenda, and frequently each has endeavoured to ascribe to itself total autonomy. Yet within each sphere there are atomist divisions. Commercial, political, transport and industrial interests impinge on strategic decision-making. At the tactical level there are the diversified criteria of traffic engineers, conservationists, planners and architects to be considered.

Altogether it might appear that the problems are so complex as to defeat any attempt at wholist design. Whilst not admitting this, it must certainly be conceded that a design and organizational talent of exceptional calibre is required to assimilate all sectional interests and mandatory conditions and weld them into a solution that rises to the level of urban excellence.

If dynamic and mind-enhancing townscape is to be moulded from such complex and sometimes intractible raw material as a contemporary planning agenda, the ultimate decisions must be taken by a spatially-orientated designer.

Ultimately, what matters to people in towns and cities is the phenomenology of buildings, roads, piazzas, gardens and monuments. All strategic and planning factors should focus down to this level of significance. Urgently needed are men who can make poetry out of such mundane raw materials. Much more than in Renaissance times, we need *uomo universale*.

References

1 A. R. Luria, *The Working Brain*, Penguin Books (1973), pp. 78–9, and R. E. Ornstein, *The Psychology of Consciousness*, Chap. 3, W. H. Freeman (1972)
2 A finding described by Professor Sir John Eccles in a lecture 'Brain, Speech and Consciousness', 1972.

22 The Nature of Innovation

Understandably in such technology-intensive times there is a growing tendency to adopt an exclusively systems approach to design. Inevitably, a mechanistic design philosophy produces inhuman urban environment. But this is not an attempt to resort to polemics, but rather to suggest that a much broader approach to design strategy has a higher probability of generating a coherent, anthropomorphic and imaginative design product. Mental strategy conditions the output.

No attempt has been made to disguise the belief that current design strategy does not usually contribute to dynamic townscape. The process itself undermines creativity. This must not be confused with creativity in respect of individual buildings, of which there is a fair amount of evidence. Creative townscape, that is, environment which stimulates the mind by extending its schema of urban events, generating images and motivating exploration, is not simply a matter of imaginative architecture. It is something much more subtle and complex, involving deployment of spaces, contours, solids and voids, the building-up of a host of stimulating tensions. This is a creative challenge much greater than that which usually stems from a single building, and therefore a design strategy is needed which can open up the excitatory possibilities of a wide urban spectrum. Design is discovery, and in this context the architect/ urban designer is responsible for discovering the maximum visual possibilities latent in a given situation.

Innovation

The nature of innovation is a matter of direct concern and therefore a closer look at the anatomy of discovery is desirable. In the opening section it was suggested that the storage and retrieval system of the brain comprises patterns of cells connected by pathways. The more the connections or synapses between cells are activated the higher becomes their state of probability of excitation. Alternatively, they have a lower threshold of activation. Very quickly, as the brain develops, the system of patterns or sub-schemas of memory and their connecting routes consolidate into a coherent way of perceiving the world.

236

Clearly each individual possesses a unique system comprising innumerable experiences and impressions. However, society comprises groups from the continental scale to the nation, city, neighbourhood, street, and family. At each stage there is a residuum of experience which is common to the group, and these experiences tend to cohere in a shared manner. The system of patterns and pathways, though unique in every case, may have a broad correspondence across the group. This way the group tends to view the world in a similar way; it shares common attitudes and subscribes to the same myths and prejudices.

All this militates against creativity and accounts for the fact that novelty is often received with hostility because it contravenes group attitudes – it cuts across the consensual arrangement of patterns and connections.

Creativity is the outcome of a re-arrangement of consensual systems of patterns and connections. Novelty is constructed from that which already exists. In this sense the ancient dictum is true that there *is* nothing new under the sun. This extreme simplification contains the basic axiom that creativity is a matter of discovering new relationships between existing data patterns stored in long-term memory.

Speaking in a limited context but with wide validity, T. S. Eliot has said:

The poet's mind is in fact a receptacle for seizing and storing up numberless feelings, phrases, images, which remain there until all the particles which can unite to form a new compound are present together.[1]

Creativity is a matter of new integrations. Whether in art or science the principle is the same. In his autobiography Max Planck wrote that the innovatory scientist must have 'a vivid intuitive imagination for new ideas not generated by deduction, but *artistically* creative imagination'. Poetry is a matter of science, mathematics and art. Poincaré talks of the 'true aesthetic feeling that all real mathematicians know', a feeling derived from 'mathematical beauty . . . the harmony of numbers and forms, of geometric elegance.'

Conditions for Innovation

Creativity can only exist in a climate containing three elements. Firstly there must be sufficient quantity and diversity of information within long-term memory to make possible cortical cross-fertilization. Innovation is conditional upon there being sufficient bisociative possibilities.

A rich architectural imagination can only emerge after extensive and diverse input. Experience of architecture of all ages is a precondition of creativity in design. The teaching of architectural history in schools of architecture is at present unpopular. It is argued that historical architecture is irrelevant because now we know so much more about the whole business. Precisely, and past architecture is a good deal of what we now know. To anyone engaged in any form of creativity, nothing is irrelevant. The most constructive mind is the one which supports a fertile chaos of impressions.

Secondly, creativity is impossible without motivation. Bisociation can only occur in response to a problem. The motivation may simply arise from the stress induced by a difficult problem. When Archimedes made his famous bathroom exclamation, it was the consequence of an unconscious bisociation between a problem on his mental agenda and the displacement of water as he stepped into his bath. All conscious efforts to solve the problem of calculating the volume of an intricate crown had failed. Here was frustration – a 'blocked matrix'. Maybe motivation was increased by fear of his master's displeasure if he failed to solve the problem. The brain has no proper sense of propriety; the 'eureka' act can occur anywhere – take Martin Luther.

Thirdly, the entire system of memory and thought must be flexible. The mind which is rigid when conscious is unlikely to be creative. It is not that the unconscious mind of the inflexible personality is unable to play its underground games. Such people may dream as much as any other personality type. The blockage occurs between the unconscious and the conscious. A highly rational, deductive, unyielding mind does not offer sufficient fissures in its hard crust for the fruits of bisociation to break through. It cannot process the 'eureka' act because it does not have the perceptual tools.

So the final prerequisite for innovation is a mind which is flexible on the conscious level. This flexibility should be such as to be able to reverse all previous assumptions. Fleming's discovery of an antibiotic suitable for human consumption negated all his previous work. The ability totally to reverse his basic frame of reference is the mark of the truly great scientist.

Architecture equally has its intellectual dugouts from which protagonists defend their positions. Designers can be just as rigid as scientists or any other category of vocation. Creativity presupposes a willingness to abandon entrenched positions, to take to the wilderness and reshape the whole scheme of things.

Once again it is T. S. Eliot who sums up the situation:

... the mind of the mature poet differs from that of the immature one not precisely in any valuation of 'personality', not being necessarily more interesting, or having more to say, but rather by being a more finely perfected medium in which special or very varied feelings are at liberty to enter into new combinations.[2]

The ground has now been prepared for the presentation of a design strategy.

References

1 T. S. Eliot, *Collected Essays*, Faber and Faber (1932), p. 19
2 T. S. Eliot, *op. cit.* p. 18

23 A Design Methodology

Input and Incubation

To bring out the developmental nature of the design strategy which is being proposed, the term *iterative* design method has been chosen. This underlines the belief that the best designs are conceived in an embryonic totality at the very beginning of the design procedure. The project is developed by successive input and feedback. This is completely different from the sequential procedure of so-called scientific method, and comes close to the classic idea of artistic creativity.

There are five stages to this strategy, some of which correspond with conventional design methodology. They are:

> Input: formulation of the design agenda
> Incubation
> Conceptualization
> Development, and
> Appraisal

Input

The input comprises three categories of information:

> Non-specific or general agenda
> Regional agenda, and
> Specific agenda

It will be profitable to examine in a little detail these categories since they have a decisive effect on all design, and may amount to a formidable filter which calls for a strong nerve.

Non-specific or general agenda This comprises information common to the majority of design problems. Architecture and planning have their own general agendas which overlap at numerous points, particularly at the level of tactical design. For architects this agenda consists of the general rules of building practice and the National Building Regulations which have their equivalent in most European and Commonwealth countries and the USA. In the latter case, building control is a State matter which is nevertheless fairly uniform throughout the country.

This aspect of the design agenda should improve its efficiency with experience. Nothing teaches so well as real situations and the accumulation of such experience produces a sophisticated general agenda which operates as a 'unitary mass' when design is undertaken. One of the more tedious aspects of design education involves inculcating sufficient general agenda to make possible by the end of the course a fairly realistic design simulation exercise. It has to be committed to permanent memory, and this involves repeated exposure to the information.

Regional agenda   In Britain, urban development is closely monitored and, where necessary, controlled by local authorities with power to implement the Town and Country Planning Acts. How they operate is that officials in town halls may make recommendations to Planning Sub-Committees which in turn advise Planning Committees, whose decisions are ratified by full meetings of Council. Brave indeed are those Councillors who fly in the face of their professional advisers. The system has recently changed in favour of fewer and much larger metropolitan county councils which will have the planning powers. The idea is that they will promote more efficient strategic as well as tactical planning.

Because of the wide variety of local authorities with planning powers this system leads to remarkable inconsistencies in development control. Whole towns can reflect the prejudices and idiosyncracies of the local planning officer. A place in the south of England is achieving an increasingly flat profile. This is because the planning officer insists that no development shall be higher than the parish church. Is he a devout Anglican?

In a borough not far from the above town, the planning committee required the author to label a church with an appropriate religious symbol on the two flanking roads. This was because the normal church signals were absent. The request was refused both on theological and town planning grounds.

The Peak Park Planning Board, controlling the southern Pennines, goes so far as to publish preferred designs. This Board is one of the most autocratic likely to be encountered and establishes comprehensive conditions about materials to be used, and even architectural style. It seems to work on the assumption that any new architecture in its area is to be regretted, and some recent buildings in the district successfully live down to this axion.

Other local authority officials contribute to the Regional agenda. When it comes to deciding which official has most responsibility for conditioning the quality of urban life these days, there is room for speculation. One opinion is that many towns and cities owe their ethos to the borough Treasurer. Others are convinced the sceptre is wielded by the Engineer. The argument used to justify this is that the Engineer must be the first to make key urban decisions since his roads are related to a national network which cannot be jeopardized by the idiosyncracies of architects and planners. In Doncaster, for instance, they might have opted to keep the parish church actually inside the fabric of the town!

Specific agenda   This agenda concerns all the items which make a particular design problem unique and is determined by input from the context, whether it is small or large scale – a town in its geographical setting or a house in an established street. It includes factors concerning the specific site, such as availability of services or the nature of the micro-climate.

Finally, it must comprise the client's brief. Usually the brief is something which the architect or planner compiles from general information supplied by the client. The situation is complicated by the fact that the client body is invariably plural, and the chances of gaining acceptance for an imaginative design usually recede according to the square of the number of members of the client committee.

Committees are also prone to serial decision-making, which often means that strategic decisions are made without reference to tactical designers, and by the time the latter are called in, the die is cast.

Much has been written about methods of assembling information and establishing relationships and hierarchies, particularly by the design methodologists. The shortcoming of design method is that it attaches values to aspects of the brief and then integrates them into a rigid design model. It might be argued that a particular method of assembling and organizing information has direct architectural consequences. To counteract this tendency it is essential that the agenda should remain fluid to accommodate possible shifts of emphasis during the design procedure.

Equally important is the fact that hidden within every agenda is the personality of the designer. He unconsciously projects his hierarchy of values on the agenda. An architect who relentlessly pursues a particular image, for instance in glass and concrete, regardless of subjecting his consumers to great discomfort, is advertising a hierarchy of values which gives low priority to human beings. Many of the complaints about recent environment may be indicating that some architects are insensitive to human physical and mental needs.

Incubation

Under consideration of intuitive design it was suggested that it exploited the results of non-conscious information processing. Clearly the mind has problem-solving potential on the non-conscious plane, and therefore a design strategy which makes full use of the diverse facilities of the brain must take this into account. Extremely complex problems in mathematics and science have been solved when the significance of non-conscious processing has been recognized by the conscious, rational mind. There is no problem more complex than design in the urban context. Because of its complexity, and because it is ultimately evaluated by human beings who are anything but rational in their responses, the human mind has more chance of measuring up to the challenge than, say, the computer, provided it allows the agenda to be thrown about within the non-rational part of its system. This is why it is being proposed that an incubation period should be allocated within the design process. Being an idea of considerable importance to design strategy, the business of incubation merits some elaboration.

The remarkable thing about so much pure inventiveness in art and science is the unexpectedness with which the concept or solution arrives. Because of this phenomenon, creativity has been associated with inspiration, a term used to describe direct contact between the mind and some transcendental agency.

Whilst not denying the possibility of inspiration in this sense, it cannot be regarded as a reliable design tool for the ordinary architect. However, the concept of inspiration contains one important truth. It implies that new ideas emerge from a fundamentally different situation than arise from rational processing.

It has been stated that normal thought processes utilize the existing arrangement of patterns and connecting pathways, and that it is outside the scope of the normal role of the system to re-route connections. Yet creativity actually comprises a redistribution of pathways. The idea of inspiration has long served to explain the paradox of new insight breaking into a mental environment wholly circumscribed by natural logical or mathematical/symbolic thinking. The evidence is formidable which suggests that radical re-routing of connections *can* take place when the mind is under non-conscious executive control.

T. S. Eliot has described the process of literary creativity as being analogous to gestation and birth. The parallel is close in certain respects. It is stating that certain factors are inseminated into the mind and that these generate a wider interaction between schemas which results in new, coherent arrangements of patterns. This breaks into consciousness at the appropriate time, namely, when the new idea is sufficiently concrete to be grasped by conscious apprehension. Like many before him, Eliot recognized that poetry could not emerge from the logical, verbalized matrices to which conscious thought is committed.

The reason why the unconscious mind is so fruitful in this respect is that it is not subject to the rules which regulate consciousness. It picks up affinities that are denied to logical processing. The unconscious mind has its own criteria which create dreams and Mona Lisas. It links up Cabbages and Kings to create a new and valuable mutation, the 'Cabbing'.

This unique bisociation of hitherto unrelated patterns may seem to occur by accident. An idea may suddenly click into focus in a spontaneous way. It does this because a considerable amount of underground activity has been occurring prior to the flash of illumination. The mechanism defies understanding, but the fact is plain that the non-conscious mind is able to work purposefully to an agenda, and can produce answers which could never emerge through rational thought. Upon this level the mind has a much keener and wider sense of relatedness, recognizing points of contact between completely unconnected patterns or sub-schemas of memory. Most important, it recognizes affinity in relation to a particular need.

The creative process in terms of mathematics has been described by Henri Poincaré in a lecture which he delivered to the Societé de Psychologie in Paris. He had been concentrating for some time upon a particularly difficult mathematical problem. After a concentrated spell of fruitless effort he recounts how, after some black coffee, he had a particularly restless night. During this state of semi-awareness he describes how:

Ideas rose in crowds; I felt them collide until pairs interlocked, so to speak, making a stable combination. By the next morning I had established the existence of a class of Fuchsian functions, those which come from the hypergeometric series; I had only to write out the results, which took but a few hours.[1]

One does not need to understand Fuchsian functions to appreciate the value of this semi-dream.

Another example should be mentioned to reinforce the Poincaré description. This one is from Friedrich von Kekulé, Professor of Chemistry in Ghent. Scientifically speaking, one particular afternoon in 1865 was especially significant, because on that occasion Kekulé fell asleep. He recounts how he saw in his dream atoms 'gambolling' about and forming into rows and then twisting like snakes. Suddenly the snakes began swallowing their tales. At this he awoke, as he describes it, 'as if by a flash of lightning', for this gave him the clue to one of the most significant concepts of modern science, the discovery that certain important organic compounds are not open structures but closed chains or circles. The dream had provided an analogy for which his mind was prepared. Perhaps he was the only one at the time capable of interpreting snakes so peculiarly perverted.

The list of people attesting to a similar 'eureka' experience is considerable. Sometimes the insight comes across during sleep or reverie. At others the moment of truth can arrive whilst stepping onto a bus. Such was the context of another of Poincaré's most profound insights.

How the brain performs this wizardry remains conjecture. Poincaré had his own theory. First he was convinced of the role of the unconscious in creativity:

Most striking at first is this appearance of sudden illumination, a manifest sign of long, unconscious prior work. The role of this unconscious work in mathematical invention appears to me incontestable.[1]

He then gets to the crux of the mechanism of insight:

Among chosen combinations the most fertile will often be those formed of elements drawn from domains which are far apart . . . . Most combinations so formed would be entirely sterile; but certain among them, very rare, are the most fruitful of all.[2]

How are these 'very rare' combinations recognized and selected for presentation to consciousness? His answer is that selection is achieved by 'the aesthetic sensibility of the real creator. The useful combinations are precisely the most beautiful, I mean those best able to charm this special sensibility;'[3] so much for the Two Cultures.

Selection then is by innate sensibility. This perhaps relates to Pasteur's famous remark: 'Chance only favours invention for minds which are prepared for discoveries by patient study and persevering efforts.' This way, as Alexander Fleming modestly put it: 'One sometimes finds what one is not looking for.'

This is an essential characteristic of the creative mind, namely, the ability to conceptualize the unexpected coherence – a unique combination of patterns which have associated to form a new inevitability.

However, Poincaré's explanation is only partly satisfactory. Statistical probability is not in favour of significant re-routing of pathways occurring on a random basis. There must be a kind of executive control attuned to the needs of a specific problem, motivated by something more than 'aesthetic sensibility'.

A mind saturated in a problem keeps it on the agenda even though conscious attention may be far removed. When a problem is under conscious scrutiny, it is subject to focal awareness. The immediate problem is in sharp focus as figure against ground whilst its context shows a sharp loss-of-acuity gradient. Conscious attention therefore is only capable of considering the immediate context, that is, patterns most obviously related to the problem.

It may be that non-conscious processing is more fertile because the 'beam' of attention is no longer rapier sharp. Focal acuity is relaxed; the angle of the beam becomes much broader and covers a wider area. It embraces patterns which, under rational rules of focal awareness, would not qualify as relevant to the problem. The system by which it operates is not the rationality of the adult mind but the free-wheeling imagination of the child or the primitive. So it 'bisociates . . . frames of reference which are regarded as incompatible in the waking (or conscious) state.'[4]

245

The unconscious mind scans the cortex with a broad beam of low-intensity and searches out affinities and analogies, fulfilling according to its own rules the needs of the agenda. It takes a holist view of the problem. Lloyd Morgan was entirely right: 'Saturate yourself through and through with your subject . . . and wait.'

Saturation alone, however, is insufficient. The system of creativity by unconscious bisociation usually must be under pressure to be effective. The stress factor, emotion or feeling, is an important ingredient of artistic and scientific creativity. This seems to accelerate the scanning process and give a cutting edge to the agenda. Clearly every building cannot emerge from an intense fructification of the soul. However, the design agenda should be intensified by strong motivation to achieve the best possible solution.

The designer who is going to fulfil the contemporary agenda is the one who is a perfectionist. The perfectionist syndrome induces stress in many people, but in the architect or urban designer it is an essential aid to excellence. To cite yet again the Cathedral of the Virgin, Chartres, a great building emerged from the ashes of destruction because a masterpiece was expected. The emotional pressure of the time was a decisive factor in the design of one of the greatest buildings of all time.

Even though design offices may have to work under high pressure, it makes good sense to allocate time to the process of incubation. The mind should be allowed to perform its own peculiar alchemy. Equally important, however, is the ability to conceptualize a solution and make it work. Urban environment demands both maximum imagination and functional efficiency.

Kekulé must be allowed to sum up this chapter from an address to his learned and most rational colleagues:

Let us learn to dream, gentlemen.

References

1 H. Poincaré, quoted in Ghiselin, *The Creative Process* (1952 edition) and A. Koestler, *The Act of Creation*, p. 116
2 H. Poincaré, *op. cit.*, and A. Koestler, *op. cit.* p. 164
3 H. Poincaré, *op. cit.*, and A. Koestler, *op. cit.* p. 165
4 A. Koestler, *op. cit.* p. 164

24 The Final Straight

Conceptualization

Time is synonymous with money in the environment industry, and even the most intuitively orientated designers have to limit the period of incubation and revert to consciously directed executive control. Indeed, the gestation process can be accelerated by purposive thought, provided it is able to appreciate the non-rational rules which govern non-conscious mentation. Before discussing how this can be achieved, it will be beneficial to look at the two processing styles, in common use in architecture and planning, which may be called:

> Natural processing, and
> Logical processing

Few designers would admit to employing the first method, since it implies immaturity. Yet it is extremely common, and accounts for some of the gigantic mistakes which happen across the whole spectrum of people and nations. Natural thinking follows the uninhibited rules of the brain, that is, rules unhindered by reason. Thought freely follows the pattern of schemas and pathways laid down and maximized at a pre-rational stage of mental development. Altogether, natural processing seems to be under the direction of the limbic brain which has scant regard for logic. It is counter productive when disguised as neocortical logic.

Irrational judgements, inspired by pre-rational maximization of certain patterns and connections within long-term memory, occur even in the rarified atmosphere of architecture and planning. All decisions should be carefully analysed for irrational elements, which may be disguised as normal assumptions. Natural thinking is at the root of myths and prejudices and is therefore extremely difficult to modify.

Logical processing is more credible as a means of solving problems. Solutions to present and future problems are synthesized from past answers. In this context development consists of an extension of the past. This style of executive thought works on the principle of deduction. De Bono calls it 'vertical thinking', the facility of the mind to proceed in logical steps along low-threshold routes to a precise goal. Because of this commitment to the prevailing arrangement of information, such thinking obviously tends to inhibit discovery and innovation.

There is clearly need for a processing mode which is not incarcerated within the established pattern of schemas and pathways. If the full benefits of the freestyle processing of the non-conscious mind during incubation are to be realized, a purposive strategy is required which exhibits the same freedom of movement across the grain of established memory and thought routes. Because the primary concern is with *discovery*, an appropriate name for a liberating strategy of conceptualization is *heuristic processing*.

Heuristic Processing

The aim of heuristic processing is either to bring to a head the creative activity which has been taking place unconsciously, or force the mind which has been unproductive to get a move on.

Both Koestler and de Bono come to the conclusion that an oblique or sideways approach to a problem stands a higher chance than head-on logic of solving it. It bears repeating that creativity cannot take place within the context provided by the current arrangement of information. Development is inevitably conditioned by the *status quo* and produces at best a momentum solution. It is necessary to break free from the existing frame of reference to create the new thing. In momentum-processing, information which is not strictly relevant is excluded to produce a high-probability solution. With the heuristic style of processing, nothing is irrelevant. All information is stored for its potential value, even though it may have an extremely low probability.

This kind of executive strategy has been called 'thinking sideways' – in de Bono terms it is 'lateral thinking'. Both imply that diverting attention away from a problem may be the best way of solving it. An extension of this idea is the contention that the way to escape the momentum frame of reference to a problem is to relate it to a quite different frame of reference. In this way new bisociations are thrown up. Hidden potential within the problem is released by the unconventional method of approaching it.

The lateral approach may stimulate creativity in several ways.

1. If there is a slight degree of logical correspondence between the lateral ingredient and the existing frame of reference, then it may act both as a bridgehead to the new concept and comprise its essence; in biblical terms this embraces both the way and the truth, and verges on a momentum solution.

2. The lateral element may behave as a *catalyst*. It stimulates the interaction of memory patterns which would otherwise have no reason to combine under the self-maximizing, high-probability rules of the system. As a catalyst it is not directly involved in the new state of affairs, but has behaved in the manner of a symbol, exposing a new logic. The catalyst

may not have any connection with rational processing, and indeed may be most fruitful if it is patently absurd. Deliberate irrelevance can prove extremely relevant.

3. Another way of generating the possibility of fertile interaction is by the introduction of *chance*. This consists of injecting many extraneous ideas into the design equation in the hope that a chance interaction may prove fruitful. If enough ideas are mixed together there is the possibility of discovering the hidden components of a new bisociation. The unconscious mind conducts its scanning operation, especially when attention is directed elsewhere, and with luck a new affinity will be revealed.

4. A useful dictum for designers was proposed by Souriau: 'to invent you must think aside'. Once one has become saturated in the problem it is then frequently productive to direct attention elsewhere to allow the unconscious mind free reign. This is a common technique with regard to memory recall. A particular memory may elude determined conscious recall, then shortly after attention has moved elsewhere the memory pattern leaps into consciousness. In design terms this may be achieved by developing two situations in parallel, each providing creative diversion for the other. It is better still if attention can be directed to something entirely outside the context of the problem. In a sense, this procedure is really an extension of incubation.

5. Unexpected possibilities may be opened by the lateral use of semantics. The elements of the problem may be defined by adjectives appropriate to an entirely different context. This is an activity best employed by a group. In the design sphere, group strategies for liberating ideas are now quite common, such as games simulation and brainstorming.

6. A further technique for seeing a problem in a new light is to change the point of entry into the problem. In design terms the very fact that there is a fairly standard sequence of actions can predetermine a type of

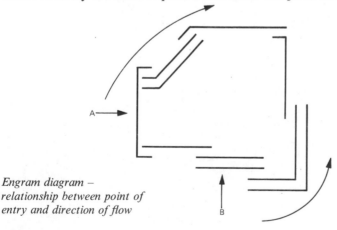

Engram diagram –
relationship between point of
entry and direction of flow

solution. In terms of engram notation, the direction of the flow of thought is determined according to where the problem is taken up. The direction of flow is regulated by the degree of maximization of schemas and pathways.

Entering the problem at point A conditions the way it is processed by logical thought. But if it is tackled from point B, the maximization rule causes attention to flow in the opposite direction. The priorities for a re-development plan can look very different from the standpoint of, say, a postman.

7. Yet another emancipating technique is to reverse the roles of figure and ground. Objects take on meaning because they stand out against a background. If the background is perceived as the dominant, surprising things can happen.

8. Finally, those who can achieve a state of meditation may be able to simulate a penumbral, dreamlike state in which attention flows freely across virgin territory in the mind, uncharted by pathways, but in the context of a firm agenda. It is not suggested that this state should be artificially induced, despite such exemplars as Samuel Taylor Coleridge. The writer does all basic architectural designing in front of the television set; this is an excellent substitute for drugs!

For the fruits of non-conscious gestation to be exploitable by the conscious mind, certain conditions are necessary. The creative mind is one which is able to accommodate radical shifts in its frames of reference. It quickly tires of clichés and searches for the unexpected in the seemingly obvious. The mind that is committed to a logical arrangement of information will never be creative; there is nothing so infertile as the strictly logical mind which is always right. De Bono offers a text for all architects and designers:

It is better to have enough ideas for some of them to be wrong than to be always right by having no ideas at all.

Development

The design which has been conceived during incubation and extracted by conceptualization techniques has to be capable of development into a building which works. More routine tasks now have to monopolize the design procedure. The process becomes one of a reciprocal sequence of development and feedback. Figuratively, the movement towards the final design follows the path of a helix.

This is the time for the exploitation of the mental facility which causes the mind to be logical, the *consistency-demand*. This is the tendency of the mind, which operates both in perception and thought, to fit data into patterns of internal affinity. The primary concern is with the rules of the game. Once again it is the non-conscious mind which performs this sophisticated processing role by strictly applying the rules of the particular system under consideration. One of the most demanding things about architectural design is that a single decision, which may initially seem trivial, can have innumerable repercussions throughout such things as structure and services. In one respect the mind operates skills equivalent to a computer, and possibly this is the point at which the computer has greatest potential.

To make the most of this consistency facility of the mind, the rules of the game have to be firmly implanted. Only when a comprehensive system of rules is installed in permanent memory can this automatic feedback system operate and test the whole design complex for inconsistencies each time a decision is made. Incompatibilities are thrown-up either in coherent form or through a sense of unease in the mind, leaving conscious executive control to discover the point of illogicality. Lesser mortals need check-lists.

It is important that through the lengthy and mundane process of development, the original vision is retained. Despite the formidable technical specification behind modern design, the product must not only be a machine for modifying microclimate but also a thing of elegance.

Appraisal

Maybe the most difficult skill for the architect to acquire is the facility to criticize his product with true objectivity. He must achieve what T. S. Eliot would have considered impossible, the ability to be both artist and critic. Right through the design process, the critical faculty is always active. Even so, a rigorous intensification of criticism is required after development is thought to be complete. Perhaps it is only at this stage, after innumerable small mistakes have been avoided, that a grand fallacy becomes apparent. Holistic appraisal is essential; the moment of truth for the right cerebral hemisphere.

Actually there must be an animated dialogue between the two hemispheres of the neocortex, since holist appraisal is most efficient when related to semantics. Architects are sometimes accused of being inarticulate, and at times even illiterate. This is a great pity, since critical ability is closely linked to semantic capacity. Thoughts rely on words to give them life. Words are the vehicles for ideas, and sophistication in the realm of analysis and appraisal is not just a matter of weighing-up the total conception, but also distinguishing subtleties and fine shades of variation. The quality of relationships and the very essence of unity and coherence may need to be verbalized before they can exist.

A command of language implies extensive powers of perception, and this is a prime skill for the urban designer, both in terms of visual input into memory and the use of memory to apply objective criteria. In design it is first necessary to clarify the design intention not only in terms of physical function but also aesthetics. It is not sufficient for so-called intuitive designers to apply vague, inchoate criteria to their designs, reduced to absurdity in the phrase: 'I know what I like.' Architects and planners must externalize their criteria, and this can only be achieved through language.

Urban architecture is the most social of all the arts. Unlike, say, Wordsworth, the architect and planner cannot enjoy the freedom to create both masterpieces and trash. A poem can be ignored; not so a building.

This has been the mere skeleton of a design strategy, in which the main purpose has been to show how certain attributes of the mind can support the operation. Apollo and Dionysius are present in different ratios in all of us, and an efficient design procedure should exploit the qualities of each at the appropriate time.

Conclusion

Undoubtedly all this will have generated many more questions that it has answered. Perhaps a good deal is controversial. Anyone stepping into the deep waters of psychology is bound to disturb sediment. It is to be hoped that a creative attitude will transcend disagreement.

This has been an attempt to make a case for a design agenda which really sets out to meet psychological needs. But not only is this plea directed towards designers; those who exercise statutory and financial control over built environment have a responsibility to recognize human needs in the urban context. This has been a description of just one way the questions of perception, design policy, and design strategy might be conceived.

Index